Renate Daniel

C.G. Jung's Analytical Psychology in Psychotherapy
Psyche and Soma
A Holistic Approach to Understanding the Mind-Body Connection

Renate Daniel

Psyche and Soma

A Holistic Approach to Understanding the Mind-Body Connection

DAIMON
Verlag

This book consists of a licensed translation and reworking of the original German edition, *Psyche und Soma: Erkenntnisse und Implikationen der Analytischen Psychologie*, © 2020 Verlag W. Kohlhammer GmbH, Stuttgart.

This English-language version was rendered by Sibylle Pot d'or and Julia Czekierska.

The author and the publisher are grateful to the *Stiftung zur Förderung der Psychologie von C.G. Jung* and the *Susan Bach Foundation*, both in Zurich, for their generous financial support of the translation and publication of this project.

Cover illustration: Wikimedia Commons.

ISBN 978-3-85630-787-5

Contents

About the author

Renate Daniel, MD, studied medicine at the University of Heidelberg and specialized in the fields of psychiatry and psychotherapy. She is a Jungian analyst, training analyst/ supervisor and Director of Programs at the C.G. Jung Institute in Zurich.

She also works as a specialist at the C.G. Jung Outpatient Clinic in Zurich, and is a member of the Scientific Management Board of the International Society of Depth Psychology (IGT) and a member of the Scientific Advisory Board of the Lindau Psychotherapy Weeks (LPTW), held annually in Germany.

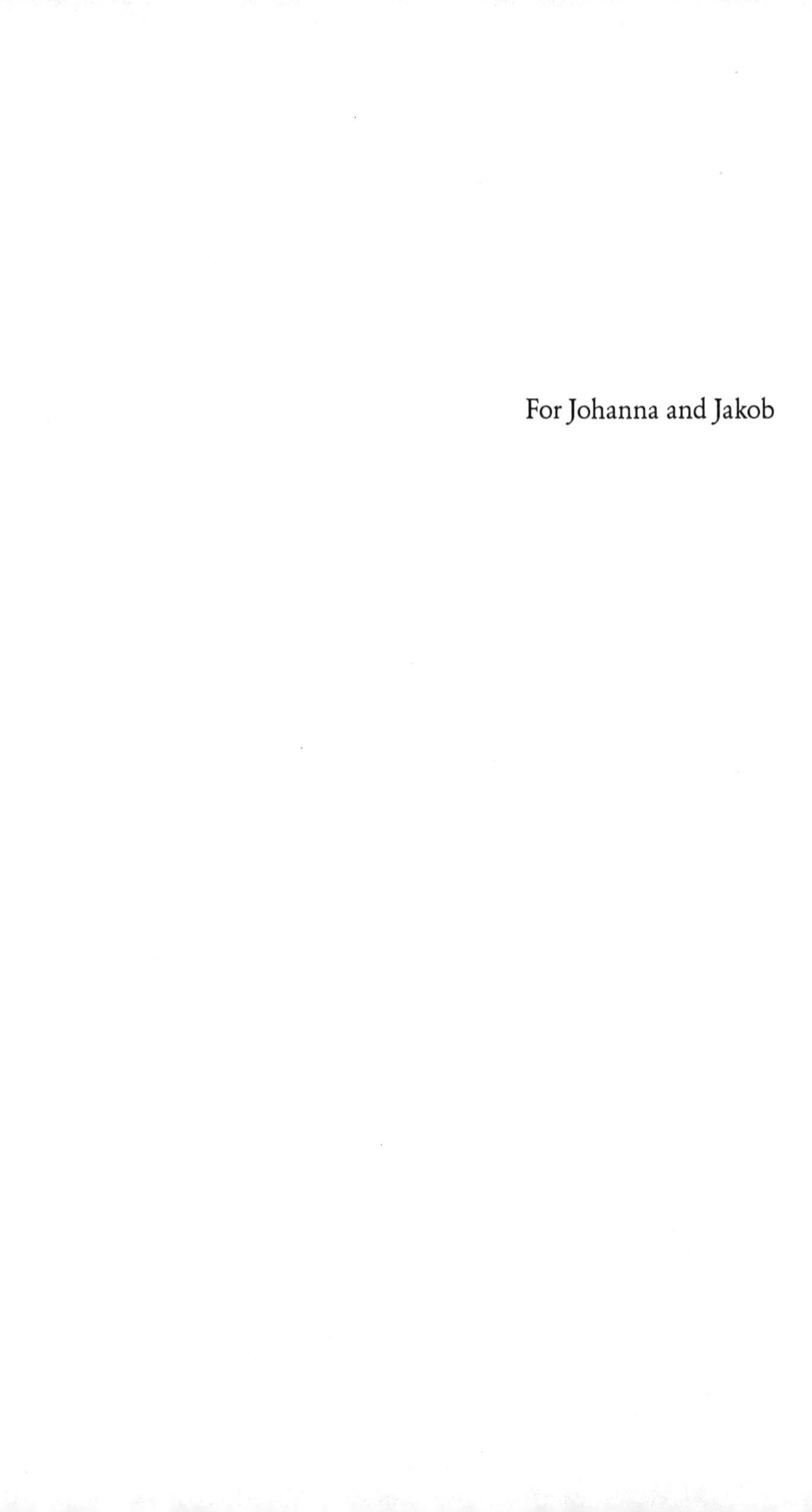

For Johanna and Jakob

Foreword

It is a pleasure to provide the foreword to this book.

Looking back at the psychotherapeutic landscape from today's standpoint, it might almost appear strange that there was a time when members of different "schools" argued vehemently about who was more successful, who had the better concept, who belonged to the mainstream, who did not, and who was of significant importance precisely because they did not belong. Meanwhile, we know from studies on psychotherapy that general factors – such as the nature of the therapeutic relationship, combined with the expectation of improvement, a patient's inner resources, and the environment in which individuals live and are treated – play a greater role than different treatment techniques. As research studies have shown (Practical Studies on Outpatient Psychotherapy (PAPs) Switzerland), therapists nowadays use many general intervention techniques in addition to school-specific ones, but above all, they employ many approaches from disciplines other than those in which they were primarily trained.

Yet, precisely because we therapists have so much in common and we are unbiased when it comes to adopting intervention techniques from other disciplines, interest is growing in what the concepts of the " respective others" really are. As a Jungian, I notice time and again that Jung's theories are used as a "quarry", whose boulders then appear in a new construction style, or in a new "setting", without reference to Jung. One example is Jungian dream interpretation, many aspects of which have been adopted whenever dream work is practiced today. The fact that C.G. Jung himself was not the first to work intensively with imagination, but that imagination is central to Jungian theory, has occasionally been "forgotten"; schema theory certainly cannot hide its proximity to Jungian complex theory, which emerged 100 years earlier.

Many conceptual overlaps may exist because Jung's original ideas are not known well enough. It is for this reason that I welcome Ralf Vogel's idea to publish a series of books, in which fundamental Jungian concepts – and their development – are described and formulated as we know them today, with a view to combining theory and practical work. I am certain that Jungian theory, in which imagery and the pictorial realm have such a great significance, can also serve as a source of inspiration for colleagues from other disciplines.

Verena Kast

Introduction

Some people are considered mentally ill, others physically ill, and still others psychosomatically ill. But is it even possible to classify patients in this way without the slightest ambiguity, and what consequences does this have for everyday life and for medical or psychotherapeutic treatment? This book aims to explore these questions on the basis of C.G. Jung's Analytical Psychology. To my mind, his empirical research findings, and the experience he accumulated in the last century are not outdated, but still provide valid inspiration for reflection on psychosomatic issues. Moreover, thanks to newer research methods available today, some of his ideas could be scientifically investigated and confirmed. Jung once formulated his stance on body and soul as follows:

> ... the human soul is not something cut off from nature. It is a natural phenomenon like any other, and its problems are just as important as the questions and riddles which are presented by the diseases of the body. Moreover there is scarcely a disease of the body in which psychic factors do not play a part, just as physical ones have to be considered in many psychogenic disturbances. (Jung 1967, CW 13, § 195)

Based on this assessment, Jung explored various aspects of the potential interaction of body and psyche, yet without providing a systematic classification of psychosomatics. Following on from Don Kalsched's reference to the "mercurial realities" of the soul and its "quixotic, ineffable" nature that "can never be pinned down" because it is linguistically "evanescent, just out of reach" (Kalsched 2013, 22), one may doubt whether any conclusive classification can be arrived at. It would appear that regardless of the well-proven psychosomatic concepts available today, we still have to resign ourselves to accepting a certain kind of vagueness, uncertainty or inaccuracy. Neither the soul nor psychosomatics are a riddle to be solved, but a mystery to be approximated, yet never fully understood. Psyche and soma may be encircled, but their true essence will probably remain out of human reach.

This is another reason why, in view of the mind-body problem, Jung emphasized that words, terms, or concepts must not be confused with reality, that is, with the entire individual made up of psyche and body. His fundamental conviction was that in psychology, any kind of understanding can only be achieved if the realms of doing and experiencing – likewise the physis – are embraced. Hence, reality and the body will always go hand in hand. Jung holds that "the body is necessary if the unconscious is not to have destructive effects on the ego-consciousness, for it is the body that gives bounds to the personality" (Jung 1969, CW 16, § 503), and "without the body, the soul is unreal" (Jung 1967, CW 13, § 316).

Interestingly enough, in 1958, three years before his death, Jung urged people to take to heart the following viewpoint expressed by the Dutch poet Eduard Douwes Dekker, writing under the pseudonym Multatuli: "Nothing is completely true and even that is not completely true", adding that "every sentence in psychology can be turned around and would still be true" (Youtube; C.G. Jung answers questions 4/6, 1958). In view of the many unanswered questions, theories or examples presented here, approaching this book with a similar attitude will enable readers to accept the contradictions that might arise in this context as practically inevitable.

1.

Empirical Research on the Interaction of Psyche and Body

1.1 C.G. Jung's Word Association Studies – Emotion, Imagination, and the Body

In 1903, during his residency at the Psychiatric University Hospital in Zurich, C.G. Jung began research which provided important clues to the interrelationship between body and psyche. His interest was not initially centered on the mind-body connection, but on psychic regularities in healthy people. In order to find out what was going on in their minds, Jung and his colleagues conducted numerous empirical word association studies. These consisted of a total of one hundred individual words that were called out successively to healthy test subjects, ranging from rather neutral words such as table, month, or glass, to ones like death, pride or lie. The subjects were then asked to say the first thing that came to mind as quickly as possible. The respective association was noted down and, in addition, the reaction time was measured between the word in question and the response. In the second, so-called reproduction phase of the experiment, all one hundred words were read out again individually to the subjects, who were asked to recall the responses they had given. Correct or incorrect reproductions were also documented.

This word association test was not new back in 1903, but unlike earlier researchers, Jung was the first to be interested in so-called interferences, as inconsistent spontaneous responses were evident in all test subjects. Sometimes, their answers followed after some hesitation, other times they would misspeak, repeat the called-out word, give multi-word responses or simply gesture, to name but a few conspicuous features. Interestingly, such disturbances were coherent and a chaotic pattern was not discernible in any one person. By means of numerous examples, Jung was in fact able to reveal an inherent logic in these disturbances. In one instance, a subject responded with great hesitance to the terms *water*, *ship*, *lake*, and *swim* and, moreover, did not remember any of his answers correctly. The debriefing revealed that during a desperate phase of his life, he had contemplated suicide by drowning (Jung 1972, CW 2, § 743ff), and these four words thus helped to reveal a personally significant and highly emotional issue. Jung called these emotionally relevant subject areas "feeling-toned complexes".

He defined a complex as an entity of several interwoven components, consisting of the accumulation of experiences, relationships and thematic ideas in a person's memory. In the case of the mother complex, this would be comprised of personal episodes, images, thoughts, beliefs, or perceptions of motherliness, which make up the relationship with our biological mothers, but also the experiences we have of other persons or life situations which we perceive as being maternal. Such complex images and experiences are inseparably linked to emotions, indeed a whole range of them. Basically, human complexes are not of a pathological nature, but are normal structures of the psyche, comparable to physical organs. In the same way that these can be healthy or diseased to varying degrees, complexes may likewise be affected.

After discovering the complexes, Jung wanted to better understand the connection between complex reactions and the body, which is why he started measuring several physical parameters during word association tests, namely breathing, pulse and electrical skin conductivity, also called skin resistance. The latter depends on sweat gland activity and is controlled by the sympathetic nerve of the autonomic nervous system. This had already been at the focus of investigations by Zurich neurologist Otto Veraguth a few months earlier, when he had read out texts to test subjects and found that skin conductivity always changed during emotional text passages. Everyday words did not evoke any response, whereas words that triggered a sufficiently intense emotional reaction led to a change in skin conductivity (Jung 1972, CW 2, § 1043), meaning that subjects would start sweating as soon as they became emotionally aroused.

Based on these and his own empirical investigations using the word association test, Jung concluded that all emotional processes influence skin conductivity to a greater or lesser extent (Jung 1972, CW 2, § 1080). Each word that leads to a complex and gives rise to an emotion, alters the electrical conductivity of the skin and does so in direct proportion to the emotional vibrancy (Jung 1972, CW 2, § 1048). Hence, complexes are not mere emotional and mental phenomena, but always anchored in the body as psychosomatic entities. By measuring skin conductivity, it became possible to capture the physical counterpart of feelings in an objective manner, as the level of arousal in the autonomic nervous system was reflected in the growth curve of the measuring device, the so-called galvanometer.

Jung also took an interest in the effect that emotions have on breathing and observed that emotional tension tends to cause shallow and increased breathing, whereas relaxation tends to slow down and deepen it (Jung 1972, CW 2, § 1062). Many people are unaware of the fact that every emotion – such as fear, anger, sadness, or happiness – leads to changes in breathing patterns. However, Jung's findings show that emotions are not as closely and deeply connected to the respiratory function as they are to the sweat gland system, which is not surprising. Breathing may quite easily be influenced via consciousness, which is why it can be used in respiratory therapy. Sweat secretion, on the other hand, is not regulated by conscious control (Jung 1972, CW 2, § 1062). The autonomy of the sweat response may have been the reason why skin resistance was admitted as evidence that a person was telling the truth or lying in so-called lie detector tests. To my mind, the results of Veraguth and Jung simply prove that a lie detector can show the presence of an emotional arousal when the subject is sweating, but not which topic or complex this arousal is triggered by. Careful questioning is needed to identify the complexes and thus, the psychological background of a vegetative reaction such as this. Sweating may not only be triggered by lies, but also by complex topics that are linked to feelings, such as shame, fear, or powerlessness. Conversely, individuals who are not emotionally aroused when they lie, e.g., because they have no feelings of guilt, will not show a vegetative reaction and no vibration amplitude will be observed in the measuring device.

Back in 1890, before Jung and Veraguth's time, Russian physiologist Ivan R. Tarchanoff had already measured changes in the skin resistance of his subjects when tickling them on the face or the soles of their feet with a feather. He then proceeded to simply forewarn his subjects about impending touches and observed that even this led to measurement deflections. His curiosity now aroused, he asked the test persons to recall feelings of anxiety, fear, or joy, which were likewise reflected by the device. When his subjects were engaged in abstract work, however, such as solving math problems, there were no measurement deflections. Tarchanoff's findings thus also indicated a connection between inner images, emotions, and bodily phenomena (Jung 1972, CW 2, § 1040).

Inspired by Tarchanoff's study designs, Jung investigated whether pricking someone with a needle or merely announcing one's intention to do so would make a difference. Pricking a subject with a needle, that is, inflicting pain, leads to changes in skin resistance and will induce sweating. A similar intensity in skin resistance change occurs when merely announcing the stimulus, as the body reacts to the emotional arousal of expectations, fantasies, and imagination. No direct touch is necessary. Emotions triggered by imagination will affect the body. These relatively simple technical measurements carried out in the 20th century illustrate how easily people can be retraumatized. As soon as a word or an involuntarily emerging inner image triggers emotions, the autonomic nervous system is aroused and more or less autonomic physical arousal processes take place, which are simply stress responses. However, these results are important not only for traumatic memories, but for all (psychotherapeutic) conversations that generate emotions. Every word capable of triggering an emotion affects the body via the autonomic nervous system. In people whose emotions are easily triggered, the autonomic nervous system jumps into action quite quickly. Thinking of the word association test as a standardized telegram-like dialogue, it becomes clear that everyday conversations can likewise be regarded as constant encounters with emotional complexes. As soon as uncomfortable questions come up, or a delicate or embarrassing topic is touched upon in conversation, disturbances occur similar to those in the word association test. Experience has shown that a single stimulus word may suffice to expose us mercilessly to a complex. The further course of events is likewise subject to autonomous processes: we no longer react freely and confidently, but in an inhibited, embarrassed, irritated, perhaps even in a verbally abusive or physically aggressive – often exaggerated – manner. Even if we manage to remain outwardly calm, an eye twitch, a tremor, a facial flush, a paleness in appearance, or a change in voice may indicate that a complex has been touched upon.

Whenever this happens, we not only react by displaying inappropriate emotions, but quite often fall into familiar behavior patterns because past experiences rush to the surface. It would appear as if the memory box were being opened and old patterns of thinking and behavior reactivated, regardless of whether they are appropriate in the given situation or not. We project former patterns of experience onto the current situation without verifying whether they are adequate in the now. Brian Broom assumes that emotional schemas – or *complexes* in Analytical Psychology – are stored in the unconscious at three different levels. At the first memory level, experiences are stored as sub-symbolic physical states, that is, embodied. Above this is the second, symbolic-nonverbal level of imagery, and at the very top, the symbolic language level. In his view, human experiences are encoded equally on all three levels: body – image – language (Broom 2015). None of these levels will ever repulse the other two, but represents one facet of human existence. Edward Whitmont shares this view, adding that therapeutic access can most likely be facilitated when the very level that houses the complex in question is touched. In his opinion, early, pre-linguistic emotional experiences therefore require body-oriented therapies because these experiences are anchored in the body memory – still without images (Whitmont 1993, 63f). However, according to what has been said so far, it is obvious that working on emotions or on emotional regulation in the context of verbal psychotherapy already leads to an initial "contact" with the body. Painting therapy or sandplay therapy are even more physical in that they provide materials with which the body creates two- or three-dimensional artefacts. Actual touching during body therapy is even more intimate and physical.

Today, going to a laboratory to measure the bodily functions described above is no longer required. Thanks to modern technology, lay people have been able to examine the described interrelationship between their body, mind, and emotions under everyday conditions for quite some years. One of them is four-year-old Felix, who developed early-onset diabetes, and was fitted with measuring devices to monitor his blood glucose, heartbeat, skin resistance and movement activity. In parallel, each meal he ate was written down, as was his physical and mental state. When he started preschool, the data analysis revealed that his blood sugar level was particularly high on Tuesday mornings, even though he had the same breakfast every day. It turned out that Felix was afraid of a teacher who taught classes every Tuesday morning, and this stressful emotion increased his blood sugar level (Kucklick 2014, 12), making the connection between anxiety and blood sugar metabolism evident. Emotions – and thus, complexes – have an impact on many bodily regulatory circuits, which can today be measured and objectified in an increasingly differentiated manner. In Felix's case, an authority complex may have been at play.

1.2 Placebo Research – Expectation, Hope and the Body

The mind-body-emotion interaction, and that of mental activity and physiology, are also to be found at the forefront of placebo research investigations. What happens when people take "drugs" which do not contain a pharmacological substance? Nowadays we know that the positive expectations a patient attaches to treatment predetermines whether a placebo effect will occur or not, and if so, how powerful this will be (Benedetti 2014, 22). The basic prerequisite for a placebo effect therefore is that the patient knows what effects the alleged medication will have and indeed expects to benefit from.

Most findings on the effects of placebos stem from pain research. Numerous neurobiological studies have shown that placebos relieve pain primarily via the dopaminergic reward system and the brain's own morphine system. In about 35% of cases, they have the same effect as morphine, with brain activity primarily involving the limbic system, which is the region that plays an important role in emotional processes (Benedetti 2014, 109).

In the limbic system, sensory information – including pain – is evaluated on an emotional basis. Unconsciously, pain and other perceptions are correlated with our current mood, past experience, and personal attitudes. In the language of Analytical Psychology, this unconscious correlation thus refers to our complexes. The information is then passed on to the prefrontal cortex, the area of the human cerebral cortex responsible for the conscious interpretation of signals. In the prefrontal cortex, neuronal activity increases more markedly the more convinced subjects are that their pain will be relieved by the placebo. Thus, the prefrontal cortex plays a major role in the placebo effect. Whereas today's research can observe the brain at work, this was not possible 100 years ago. Jung and other researchers could only measure peripheral physical changes, such as sweat secretion, respiration, and pulse rate. But their findings already pointed in the direction described above, namely that imagination is a mental, emotional, and physical phenomenon. The word "tajassom", meaning both "to embody" and "to imagine", has long born testimony to this in the Persian language.

It is currently considered a proven fact that the antidepressant Fluoxetine acts in the same brain regions and in a similar manner to placebos administered for depression. Likewise, placebos for pain trigger changes in brain activity patterns similar to those seen in treatments with opioid painkillers. It is hardly surprising then that Naloxone, as an opioid antagonist, not only reverses the effects of analgesics, but also the analgesic effects of placebos (Benedetti 2014, 186).

Despite all these overlaps, differences should not be overlooked. Opioid-containing medication also activates brain regions that placebos have no effect on. For some, this explains why the effect of placebos diminishes over time, while painkillers retain their efficacy. However, this loss of efficacy could also have psychological reasons, at least to some extent. After all, Jung had found in the word association tests that the repetition of images usually leads to less intense physical reactions, which he understood as an exhaustion of the stimulus (Jung 1972, CW 2, § 1056). "Dwindling excitement", i.e., diminishing emotional involvement, such as lack of interest or boredom, will weaken the effect. When a placebo is administered and taking pills becomes a daily routine, it usually ceases to be a particularly exciting affair. This could explain why the effectiveness of a placebo diminishes, because the intensity of the emotional arousal that was triggered plays a decisive role in the placebo effect.

Thus, the more intensely positive emotions are generated, the more likely it is that the hoped-for physical effect will occur. The greater the impression left by an environment, a ritual, a setting or a therapy method, the more positive projections it results in, and the higher the probability that a placebo effect will take place. Hence, the administration of small white pills tends to have a lower placebo effect than the prescription of colorful capsules, injections, or impressive procedures. If a painkiller is, e.g., administered by the chief physician, it may have a longer-lasting effect than if injected by a medical assistant.

Previous findings show that expectation and faith are at the foundation of the placebo effect, which is indeed not "imagination", but a real, material phenomenon. A material manifestation takes place in the body, which is why the placebo effect should not be scorned at as something illusory or unreal. The more hope a doctor, a therapist, or even an exotic-looking ritual or procedure can inspire, the greater the likelihood of a physical effect. This phenomenon could also play an important role in the use of "questionable" methods. If someone has confidence in and can project hope onto obscure or seemingly absurd methods, or place trust in so-called quacks, charlatans or frauds, a material reaction may occur.

In this context, Jung's reference to the appeal of novelty is interesting. He understands novelty as an emotionally arousing situation which may be accompanied by the expectation of a miracle. Novelty and the unknown seem particularly apt stimuli for positive future projections, and placebo research has revealed that such expectations can give rise to a material manifestation, insofar as interest is sustained. Such was the case of a patient who, faced with very advanced metastatic lymphosarcoma, had only a few days to live from a medical point of view. But unlike his doctors, the patient was full of hope because he had heard about a new drug that was about to enter the clinical trial market in the forthcoming days. He was so enthusiastic about this drug that he managed to convince the attending physician to include him in the study, although his poor physical condition would have ruled him out of participation. A few days after receiving the first shot of the drug, an incredible improvement in his general condition was to be observed, and the tumors and metastases had regressed to half their size. He was the only patient to exhibit such a positive healing process and within the space of a few weeks, he was completely cured. Subsequently, he remained symptom-free and had no physical ailments for two months. However, after learning through the news that the administered drug was said to be completely ineffective, he lost all hope and faith, suffered a relapse, and died a few days later (Whitmont 1993, 65ff).

Similar in pattern, but less spectacular, is the case of a 40-year-old architect who had repeatedly suffered from depressive episodes over a period of several years. Each time, she had taken the same antidepressant which had quickly shown a very positive effect. One day, after the patient had stumbled across a study on the Internet about the alleged ineffectiveness of the drug, she began to have her doubts, and a few days later the drug lost its beneficial effect. The doctor's rational explanation, namely that the study was in no way correlated to her own personal experience and of no specific relevance, as it had merely drawn a statistical conclusion, did not help either and she had to discontinue the drug.

In situations where one person is convinced of the effectiveness of and believes in the healing power of a drug, while another person does not, bitter disputes can arise. The question as to which view is correct cannot be answered as such, because belief is not something that is decided upon voluntarily by the ego and every belief, no matter how bizarre, may result in a material effect. If one person believes in something and the other does not, they are in reality living in two seemingly unbridgeable, different worlds. However, one can safely say that the "non-believer" will not experience any material, i.e., physical effect.

If it is true to say that patients must understand the purpose of the particular substance they are taking, and that their prior expectations in this relation must be positive in order for a placebo effect to occur, then it holds that people suffering from dementia will have a significantly lower response rate to placebos. This is indeed the case, as people suffering from Alzheimer's need higher doses of painkillers (Benedetti 2014, 136). It is also due to the significant contribution that the placebo effect has on the effectiveness of "real" drugs. Some of them at least do not develop their full healing potential if applied covertly, as proven by experiments in which patients were not informed about the effect of the pharmaceutical substances they were receiving. This was demonstrated, among other things, by a study conducted by neurologist Ulrike Bingel on the opioid Remifentanil. For this purpose, she inflicted a defined pain on healthy patients, the intensity of which was assessed by the subjects on a scale ranging from 0-100. On average, pain intensity was rated at 66. All subjects were attached to an infusion and the pain medication fluid was administered in three different drip settings. In one experiment, subjects were not informed that the opioid was already present in the infusion. Pain intensity decreased to an average of 55, showing that the drug had had the expected effect. In the second experiment, subjects were informed that they would receive a painkiller via the infusion. In this case, pain intensity was reported to be 39, although the same dose of the opioid was used as in the first experiment. Thus, apprising subjects of the beneficial effects to be expected significantly enhanced pain relief. In a third series of experiments, study participants were informed that the analgesic would no longer be administered and that they could therefore expect to experience a higher level of pain. This was not true, however, as they continued to receive the same dose of the opioid. In this scenario, the subjects described their pain as having an intensity level of 64 points (Schubert/Amberger 2019, 227f), showing that their internal anticipation had again produced a considerable physical effect. These phenomena have been documented not only with analgesics, but also with anxiolytics. When given without reference to their anxiety-reducing effects, they prove to be significantly less effective (Benedetti 2014, 186). Thus, if a chemical substance is ingested, both substance-related and mental-emotional factors are always involved in its effect, albeit to varying degrees, which should be taken into account.

Since it has been shown that the placebo effect plays a contributory factor in the administration of chemical substances, we should consider whether patients who exhibit a strong emotional resistance should receive them. Indeed, there is reason enough to expect that not only positive thinking, but also concerns may materialize and some studies point in this direction. It has been proven that, e.g., anxious apprehension increases pain by deactivating dopaminergic and opioid systems (Benedetti 2014, 148). This is referred to as the nocebo effect, which is derived from the Latin word *nocebo = I will harm*. Destructive, negative thoughts about the drug may take root in the body, and those facing a scheduled treatment with great apprehension, trepidation or fear have a higher probability of the therapy developing in the way they imagined – a phenomenon known as *self-fulfilling prophecy*.

Physical reactions to internal representations, mental images, and emotions are objectively measurable today, but are assumed to have existed for a long time. As early as around 440 B.C., the Greek physician Hippocrates expressed the notion that besides environmental influences, nutrition or insufficient excretion, a misdirected affect balance could cause physical illnesses. From his understanding, the art of healing was first and foremost a science of proportion, which included the treatment of affects. About 300 years later, similar assumptions were expressed by Galen, who also worked in Greece. He considered the diagnosis of affects essential in the treatment of all disease (Schipperges 1999, 31f, 38). In the 13th century, theologians Albertus Magnus and Thomas Aquinas were convinced that the imaginative power of the soul could bring about tangible changes in the material world during states of high affective tension. They believed the human soul to be capable of changing real things when carried away by great excesses of love, hate, or some other passion. As soon as the soul is gripped with an intense desire, it becomes materially effective (Jung 1969, CW 8, § 859). The Dutchman Boerhaave (1668-1738), celebrated as the best physician and chemist of his time, also postulated that violent or prolonged emotional states of the soul could alter, paralyze, or corrupt the brain, muscles, and organs, and promote or give rise to disease (Meier 1994, 215). The existence of a mind-body interaction appears to have been accepted for quite a long time, but how exactly does it manifest itself?

1.3 Psychoneuroimmunology – Stress, Emotion, and the Immune System

The field of psychoneuroimmunology also explores mind-body interactions, and has fostered an even greater understanding of the fundamental processes involved. The upswing in this discipline began around 1970, when researchers increasingly turned their attention to the question of whether and how psychological or psychosocial factors affect the nervous, hormonal, and immune systems, and vice versa.

In 1975, an experiment carried out by Robert Ader and his team caused quite a sensation: A toxically active cytostatic drug (cyclophosphamide) in a sugar solution (saccharin) was administered to rats. Such cytostatic drugs are used in chemotherapy because they inhibit cell division and the growth of cancer cells. On the downside, they also inhibit the division and proliferation of healthy cells, which – among other things – results in the production of fewer red and white blood cells in bone marrow.

Since white blood cells form a cornerstone of defense in our immune system, a cytostatic treatment will normally also weaken our resistance, resulting in less effective anti-pathogen defense mechanisms. And an insufficient immune response can cause an otherwise harmless infection to become quite threatening.

This side effect of cytostatics was already known at the time of Ader's experiment, so the research team was not surprised – and had in fact expected – that the rats would react to the administered cytostatic drug with immunosuppression. In the second part of the experiment, the rats were administered only the sugar solution, which had an unpleasant bitter metallic aftertaste. Although the rats were now only ingesting this bad-tasting, but medically "harmless" substance, their immune systems often reacted disproportionately and – depending on the sugar dose – with sometimes life-threatening immunosuppression. It was assumed that the animals had made a connection between the immunosuppressive drug and the taste experience (Schubert 2015b, 5). Repeated, unpleasant experiences thus affected the rats' immune systems, a fact which is reminiscent of the influence of expectations in the aforementioned placebo effect: the animals' endogenous immune system had reacted although they had not ingested any immune-boosting substance. This goes to show that a repeated, emotionally unpleasant experience can induce an immune response.

Under stress, the organism reacts to different internal and external stimuli (stressors), while trying to cope with the demands at hand. From a depth psychology point of view, these stressors can activate complexes as well as trigger internal images, emotions, and physical phenomena. There is consensus among psychoneuroimmunologists that psychological or physical challenges, in the form of acute or chronic stress, trigger a cascade of biological processes in humans. The stress response leads to messenger substances, such as norepinephrine, epinephrine, and cortisol, being released from the adrenal cortex to modulate the body's innate and acquired immune defense. Chronic stress and the subsequent release of elevated levels of cortisol can lead to increased susceptibility to infection, as cortisol inhibits immune activity. It can also lead to obesity, lack of sleep, or impaired memory – symptoms known to occur when there is an excess production of cortisol (Marlakey, Tafur, Rutledge & Mills 2015, 45).

Yet, the psyche has not only damaging, but also positive effects on the immune system. Numerous research studies confirm that psychotherapy can downregulate excessive cortisol levels, and in this way, improve maladaptive physiological immune processes (Malarkey et al. 2015, 40f). It has been proven that working on our complexes, i.e., improving emotional regulation and dysfunctional beliefs, has a positive effect on the immune system's regulatory processes. Furthermore, pleasant physical sensations, such as tender touches, massages, and the experience of emotional security, have a positive effect on the immune system and are known to reduce cortisol levels.

In this context, it should not be forgotten that whether chronic stress is detrimental to a person's health or not, and to what extent, depends on the cognitive assessment and the emotional arousal of the affected individual (Picardi, Tarsitani, Tarolla & Biondi 2015, 143). Experiencing stress as a challenge, a call, an incentive, or an opportunity will lead to different physiological reactions than those that feelings of being overwhelmed by a stressor would lead to.

Digression: The Immune System

The task of our immune system is to recognize and remove foreign substances, such as viruses, bacteria, parasites, or antigens (foreign protein). To ensure survival, the immune system has a variety of cell types, messenger substances and proteins (interleukins, cytokines, interferon, etc.) at its disposal. These mature, differentiate and reside mainly in the bone marrow, the thymus, the lymph nodes, or the spleen. As soon as they are needed elsewhere, they start to migrate.

An effective immune response is achieved through the cooperation and coordination of the innate and the acquired immune system. The *innate* immune system attacks foreign bacteria, viruses, but also cancer cells with granulocytes, macrophages, or natural killer cells. It stands ready within hours as a non-specific defense. The specialized *acquired* immune system, on the other hand, needs days to react because it produces specific antibodies for a specific antigen. At the same time, this specific antigen is anchored in the immunological memory, which is why the acquired immune system can react more quickly when coming back into contact with this specific antigen. Vaccinations make use of this memory process, for example.

The acquired immune system includes T-lymphocytes developed in the bone marrow, which differentiate into subpopulations in the thymus. In this way, so-called T helper cells TH1 are produced, which initiate inflammatory processes, i.e., have a pro-inflammatory effect. T-helper cells TH2, on the other hand, are tasked with attenuating inflammation, thereby producing an anti-inflammatory effect. The thymus also verifies whether these TH1 and TH2 cells recognize the body's own structures. Should this be the case – which is about 95% of the time – these cells must be destroyed, because they would otherwise attack the body's own tissue. This cell destruction is a necessary protective measure against autoimmune diseases.

As soon as an antigen encounters a suitable T-helper cell, the latter starts searching for a matching B-lymphocyte, which is also part of the acquired immune system and developed in the bone marrow. After the B-lymphocyte and T-lymphocyte have met, the B-lymphocyte clones itself and the resulting identical B-cells now begin to produce one and the same antibody, which is in turn needed for the targeted combat of the specific antigen.

In a healthy organism, complex regulatory mechanisms prevent premature, inappropriate, or exaggerated immune responses. They are also responsible for balancing inflammatory processes, set in motion by any defense reaction involving swelling, redness, and tissue changes. Acute inflammation will turn into chronic inflammation if the immunocompetent cells are not shut down by these regulatory mechanisms (Niggermann & Zänker 2015, 50-67).

Under chronic stress, the ratio of TH1 to TH2 cells may change. People who react to stress with high cortisol levels and a lower TH1/TH2 quotient have a higher risk of developing allergies, asthma, or systemic lupus erythematosus. In contrast, those who react to stress with too weak an increase in cortisol and an elevated TH1/TH2 quotient have a higher risk of developing rheumatoid arthritis, multiple sclerosis, psoriasis, type 1 diabetes mellitus, or Crohn's disease. In all of these diseases, increased inflammatory activity is detectable (Malarkey et al. 2015, 43/Schubert 2015c, 84).

In the brain, cortisol production is regulated by the pituitary gland and part of the diencephalon, the so-called hypothalamus. The corticotropin releasing hormone (CRH) produced in the hypothalamus initially causes the release of adrenocorticotropic hormone (ACTH) from the pituitary gland, which subsequently boosts the production of cortisol under stress. In a healthy body, these three messengers balance each other out by means of feedback loops: High levels of cortisol inhibit the production of CRH.

Chronic psychosocial stress can increase blood

cortisol levels, although hypothalamic CRH levels remain normal. This is referred to as glucocorticoid resistance because the CRH in the brain no longer responds to the cortisol, meaning that the required down-regulation by cortisol becomes dysfunctional. Such a disturbed feedback mechanism (hyperresponsive system) promotes inflammation and plays a crucial role in patients with ulcerative colitis, Crohn's disease, rheumatoid arthritis, but also severe depressive disorders (Malarkey et. al. 2015, 39f).

Stress-related elevated cortisol levels due to glucocorticoid resistance can also be found in abused children. Longitudinal studies have shown that their cortisol levels, however, drop again around the age of 18 and in fact become too low, promoting inflammation (Schubert & Exenberger 2015, 121). The aforementioned psychological stress experienced during early childhood can thus promote the later occurrence of an autoimmune disease (AID) due to a maladaptive immune system. From a biological perspective, autoimmune diseases and post-traumatic stress disorder (PTSD) have many similarities, which is why psychoneuroimmunologists subsume AID and PTSD under the common label of "stress-associated diseases." Furthermore, PTSD has been shown to increase the risk of developing an AID (Schubert 2015c, 88).

Undoubtedly, there are chronic stressors that make it difficult to develop a positive inner attitude. Studies have therefore been carried out on people who struggle with the burden of caring for patients with Alzheimer's, are dealing with the stress of sitting exams, or living in toxic relationships. 8 mm artificial wounds were inflicted on these otherwise healthy subjects and a significant delay in wound healing was observed. A similar delay in healing was seen in people with poor control over anger and rage. Christian Schubert concluded that a patient's emotional state and attitude towards a forthcoming operation have a significant influence on postoperative wound healing (Schubert 2015c, 71f). From a psychological point of view, working on preoperative fears in a therapeutic setting will greatly contribute to physical healing.

In a study on susceptibility to infection, 420 healthy women and men aged 18-54 were artificially infected with pathogenic rhinoviruses to glean more information about the regulatory mechanisms of the immune system. The more stressed the subjects were at the beginning of the study, the higher their probability of contracting a cold, and the more pronounced their clinical and immunological signs of infection. It was also shown that socially well integrated subjects were less likely to develop symptoms than poorly socially integrated subjects. In the case of herpes infections, there is also a measurable correlation between chronic stress exposure and symptom reactivation. As a rule, herpes virus carriers are healthy persons, and it is their suppressed immune system – for example due to chronic stress – that leads to the manifestation of disease (Schubert 2015c, 74).

According to Schubert (Schubert 2015c, 81), these and other findings are highly relevant with regard to the spread of infectious diseases in the population. He is convinced that the increase in chronic stress in Western industrialized nations and the global financial crisis of 2008, coupled with the ensuing worldwide panic reaction, have led to immunological disorders in many people, which are partly responsible for the pandemic spread of infectious diseases. According to current knowledge, publicly stoked fear of a potentially fatal viral disease increases susceptibility to viral infection. These findings should be considered to a greater extent by decision-makers in the context of emerging infections, as in the case of COVID-19, the corona virus variant first detected in 2019.

Medical findings relating to the mind-body connection are indeed of significance when looking at collective phenomena. The steady increase of allergic and autoimmune diseases is undisputed – could collective psychological processes play a role in this context? What about human values, attitudes, and associated lifestyles? Most researchers look for material factors that trigger these diseases, as in the case of allergies, where the focus is on which antigens children come into contact with too seldom or too often. There is evidence that living on a farm tends to reduce allergic reactions, but what if psychological factors are as relevant as the animals, plants, and other antigens to which a child's organism is exposed to in such an environment? Contact with nature can lead to positive emotional experiences, which, according to the research results mentioned above, certainly have an effect on the immune system. There seems to be a growing collective consciousness that exploring nature in such an emotional way is a truly healing experience. The tourism industry has started to advertise visits to the forest – now called "forest bathing" – to promote the numerous health-boosting substances in the forest air. However, not only these material factors, but also seasonal changes, tranquility or the sounds of nature can lead to mental well-being and have a healing effect on the body.

In Analytical Psychology, we speak of nature as the archetype of the Great Mother, which, like all archetypes, is part of the so-called collective unconscious. This can be referred to as the database for the entire history of humanity, which all persons, all eras and all cultures are part of. As a physical, emotional, and mental concept, it contains typical human instincts and basic emotions, as well as imagery and imagination, handed down in myths, religion, or fairy tales. Not only Jung, but also neurobiologists, such as Mark Solms or Gerald Hüther, assume that we bring an unconscious knowledge of humanity into the world in the form of imprints that are constantly enriched by personal experience over the course of our lifetime. The collective unconscious is structured by archetypes, which can be described as emotional nodes, organized around fundamental themes, such as father, mother, child, hero, health, illness, etc. These nodes are the soul's energy centers, evidenced by the fact that they can produce fascinating or unsettling, exciting or frightening, as well as motivating or petrifying effects. As soon as the ego comes into contact with them, their effect is intense and never neutral. The range of emotions mentioned above further shows that each archetype has both positive and negative traits. In the mother archetype, these would be nurturing, cherishing, and warming versus devouring, constricting or deadly aspects. Because this unconscious knowledge of both the light and the dark poles of the mother archetype lies dormant in the unconscious, the opportunity to correct overly one-sided personal experiences lies open to us. Whosoever has had a highly destructive, personal mother experience can seek positive and healing experiences with the mother archetype through encounters with nature. It is here that one can marvel at beauty, find delight in the living, and feel connected with creation, among other things. Mother Earth gives – as long as she still can. The "Fridays for Future" movement shows how many people today feel called upon to be more protective of Mother Earth. Against many odds, the collective consciousness is beginning to change towards the need to be more maternal and caring. While planet Earth is virtually the body of all life forms, the human body can be understood as a kind of individual Earth. And just as planet Earth can be exploited more easily now because it is no longer considered as sacred, the individual body is likewise perceived as an object of use these days. As a general rule, collective attitudes are reflected in the individual, insofar as the mother archetype can not only be experienced outdoors in nature or in encounters with people, but also within the human psyche. It comes down to our ability to care for ourselves and for others.

The importance of psychological and psychosocial experiences for physical health has been demonstrated in studies of large populations, such as the large-scale Adverse Childhood Experiences (ACE) study conducted in San Diego in the 1990s. At the time, 26,824 adults were physically examined and then asked to provide information about adverse childhood experiences, such as emotional, physical, or sexual abuse, or adverse circumstances in the home (e.g., parental drug use, separation, violence, or mental illness). The study showed that early childhood trauma and related psychological stress factors, such as depression, anger, or hostility, may help explain the development of later coronary heart disease better than traditional risk factors, such as smoking, obesity, and physical activity (Schubert & Exenberger 2015, 119). Hence, a holistic psychosomatic approach not only investigates long-established risk factors, but also early, emotionally stressful experiences.

According to Schubert, these findings should not obscure the fact that the studies contain some inconsistent or contradictory statistical results, probably due to the complexity of the interaction between the psyche and the immune system. Indeed, research into mind-body phenomena is problematic because reliable observations and measurements can only be obtained from the body. In addition, standardized (laboratory) conditions are needed to be able to record and calculate statistically significant influencing factors. Rare events and thus the uniqueness of the individual, however, are of no interest to statistics which in fact even neglect or eliminate them (Jung 1969, CW 8, § 905). Yet, this is often what matters most in psychosomatics, which is why Schubert holds that further research should take a wider view of everyday human life, i.e., the subjective meaning of experiences (Schubert 2015c, 106). However, our inner world of thoughts and emotions cannot be explored by external observers – this has been and will remain a subject of very personal perception (Solms & Turnbull 2003, 77f). But precisely this realm of experience, and the significance it has in people's lives, holds the key to an overall understanding of human disease, provided that illness is not merely considered as the mechanistic result of the interaction between psyche, brain, immune system and other physical functions (Broom 2015, 364).

Of importance to note is that a two-way communication between the psyche and the immune system exists, in that psychological factors cause immunological changes and, conversely, immunological factors cause psychological changes. When the immune system fights an infection, the proteins produced for this purpose, such as interleukin 1 and 6 (IL-1 and IL-6), not only induce fever, but also loss of appetite, lassitude, and disinterest. This so-called "sickness behavior" (Niggermann & Zänker 2015, 63) is not a sign of nonspecific weakness, but a psychological set of symptoms created by the immune system, as proven by the treatment of patients suffering from chronic hepatitis or cancer. When certain cytokines were administered to support their immune system, they developed cognitive and affective symptoms, such as depression, dysphoria, anhedonia, hopelessness, concentration disorders, or exhaustion. These symptoms disappeared completely after the immunotherapy ended (Schubert 2015c, 99).

This interaction between body and soul explored by psychoneuroimmunology is reminiscent of the ancient alchemical idea of *solve et coagula = make the solid volatile and the volatile solid.* Alchemists used this to describe a cycle in which something emerges from matter and ultimately returns to it – an idea illustrated by an upright figure eight. The lower part of the eight represents the body, while the upper part stands for the spirit or the psyche. When tracing the figure eight from the bottom to the top until the intersection in the middle, one has arrived at the point of transition, where physical phenomena dissolve (*solve*) and lead to spiritual, conscious insights or emotional experiences. The metaphor continues into the upper half of the figure eight. Returning from the upper half down to the point of intersection again means approaching *coagula*, the place where the spiritual begins to materialize and takes on solid and concrete form. Visually speaking, this is the return to the lower half of the figure eight.

This kind of physical manifestation of intense emotion in the context of *coagulatio* is described by the artist Marina Abramovic in a YouTube video from 1974, in which she relates the terrible experience she had during her performance "Rhythm 0". She had given the audience the choice to inflict pleasure, joy, or pain on her body and after some time, more and more members of the audience started displaying aggressive behavior. They injured her, causing her to bleed and cry. Back at her hotel, the artist discovered a large strand of white hair in her dark head of hair – the experience of a few hours of physical and emotional distress had sufficed to let a part of her age by decades.

This phenomenon is also described in the ballad "Feet in the Fire" by Conrad Ferdinand Meyer, in which a courier of the French king is caught in a severe storm and taken in by a Huguenot. Both men realize with horror that the courier was the very person who had tortured and killed the host's wife a few years earlier. Expecting the host to take revenge, the courier spends the night in fear of death. However, the widower spares his wife's murderer, although the encounter causes his brown curly hair to turn gray overnight. Existentially disturbing emotions – mental and physical pain – touch the inner depths of the soul, inducing a rapid physical effect, as experienced by Marina Abramovic after her performance. The author of the above ballad firmly believed in this, as did the alchemists, who were also convinced that meditation and imagination were key to the transformation of physical into psychic phenomena and vice versa. Imagining was understood as a physical activity which can be integrated into the cycle of material change, can also cause such changes, and even be caused by them (Jung 1968, CW 12, § 394). How exactly this takes place in the individual, for whom this is possible and to what extent, however, still remains rather mysterious for the time being.

1.4 Relevance for Psychotherapeutic Practice

Based on current findings in psychoneuroimmunology, Christian Schubert holds that psychotherapy can intervene in dysfunctional physiological processes and in this way, cure psychosomatic illnesses (Schubert 2015b, 7). Admittedly, all those who support psychosomatic healing processes know how difficult a task this is, although we know much more about the interaction between psyche and soma today than physicians from the ancient world, alchemists in the Middle Ages, or even C.G. Jung did. Our current knowledge also proves that many of the observations, approaches or ideas of our predecessors are correct and helpful.

1.4.1 Working with Emotions

From the point of view of Jungian Psychology, a cornerstone of psychosomatic therapy is the study of complexes, i.e., early experiences, emotions, and phantasies, because they influence metabolic processes.

As soon as people have emotions, they feel energy, which usually becomes apparent on a mental and physical level. One of the possibilities for working with emotions is exemplified by an experience that C.G. Jung had, beginning in the autumn of 1913. Around that time, he was afflicted by a stream of catastrophic images surging up from the unconscious, in which he saw vast floods covering huge swathes of land stretching from England to Russia. Later, the water turned to blood, with many dead bodies lying alongside the debris. Still later, he saw the arrival of an arctic cold front in the middle of summer, causing numerous European rivers and lakes to freeze over with ice. The following year, these visions, accompanied by harrowing dreams, continued to agitate him emotionally to such a point that he often had to calm himself by practicing yoga (Jaffé 1973, 177). By using yoga exercises, Jung drew on ancient collective body knowledge and witnessed emotional regulation via the physical. Such a positive effect can, of course, be achieved not only through yoga, but also by practicing qigong, tai chi, breathing or other body therapies. The world of human emotions and the way they develop and are regulated is intimately linked to human physiology (Picardi et al. 2015, 161).

Jung described how yoga strengthened his ego and his ego complex. The calm and stability he gained enabled him to translate his distressing emotions into paintings, and to ultimately uncover the images hidden by these emotions (Jaffé 1973, 177). Jung also suggested that if he had stopped at the emotional level and not made the effort to become aware of the images behind his emotions, he would have become ill.

The three levels of body, emotion and image reflect complex experiences stored in the memory. In describing his experiences, Jung mentions how these influence each other, and how he manages to connect and remain connected to them on all three levels. Based on his own and other people's experiences, communication between these three levels, i.e., energy flowing freely between the levels in all directions, appears to be of utmost importance for mental and physical health.

In numerous people, the flow of energy between the above levels is obstructed or even cut off, making personal development or physical recovery difficult. According to Broom, this includes physically ill people who have great difficulty grasping something linguistically or connecting it with their emotions. Also affected are people who do not lack insight into their problems, but are unable to implement any concrete measures, which they often experience as disappointing and irritating. Broom explains this as a dissociation between the different levels of representation of our experiences (Broom 2015, 372). With regard to the last category, one might suspect that a person feels very much at home at the verbal-symbolic level of language and imagery, but lacks access to emotions or early, unconscious bodily experiences, so that cognition and knowledge remain at the linguistic level. It is important to note that in this context, Verena Kast points out that adults, unlike children, are adept at and familiar with desomatization. They do not act, but negotiate with themselves and others (Kast 1992, 134). As a result, adults are no longer that closely connected to, or perhaps even entirely cut off from their bodies – something that Broom refers to as dissociation.

Paying attention to "negative" emotions, such as helplessness, fear, powerlessness, resentment, anger, hatred, humiliation, or shame, is of particular importance, because these play a key role in physical and mental health. Patients and therapists alike often find negative emotions hard to cope with, which is why they tend to be avoided.

Cross-procedural psychotherapeutic research findings demonstrate how significant it is to experience and process such negative, painful emotions under therapy for treatment to be successful (Benecke 2018, 73). This is consistent with study findings in psychoneuroimmunological research. Individuals who can deal openly with negative emotionality, for example in *expressive writing*, in fact show improved wound healing, reduced Epstein-Barr virus (EBV) antibody titers and lower cortisol levels, but also higher self-esteem and better coping strategies (Horn, Mehl & große Deters 2015, 257).

Expressive writing encourages us to confront highly stressful emotions. This is a standardized method of self-disclosure where people are requested to sit alone and undisturbed in a quiet place, and write about a traumatic experience, a stressful or an extremely important emotional topic for 15 minutes (alarm clock), without interruption, on at least three or four consecutive days. Spelling, sentence structure or grammar should not be worried about, it is important that people simply focus on their innermost thoughts and feelings. Once everything has been written down about a particular topic, another theme can be chosen. It is not uncommon for people to feel sad or exhausted, or to notice an increase in blood pressure immediately after they conclude writing (Horn et al. 2015, 246). After weeks or months, any "initial aggravation" that may occur gives way to positive long-term effects, as mentioned above. Interestingly enough, expressive writing about normal, neutral, or positive topics does not result in the same strong, health-promoting effect. In terms of physiological and immunological parameters, powerful or significant effects can only be brought about by expressive writing when emotions and cognitions interfuse in the process. Writing down something from a purely emotional point of view without cognitive processing, or merely reproducing experiences on a rational level will remain ineffective. This ties in with both Jung's personal experiences as well as those of Broom and Kast, all of whom emphasized the importance of the interfusion of emotion and mind/language/image. The image serves as a basis for insight and allows people to come to terms with their situation (Kast 2016, 172).

However, disturbing emotions cannot always be dealt with directly, because the ego complex may be too fragile, there might be a strong tendency to dissociate, or massive deficits in emotional regulation exist, to name but a few examples. In such cases, and especially when someone is stuck fast in personal images, beliefs, and the associated difficult emotions, Kast recommends prioritizing opposite emotions to balance out the negative ones. When people are suffering, they should focus on joy and joyful experiences (Kast 2019, 25). These emotions can be reawakened by movement, music, but also by imagining past experiences.

1.4.2 Working with Imagination

Jung understood phantasies as an inner reality and natural expression of the unconscious life, including all autonomous body functions. He therefore believed that phantasies could contain etiological clues to physical illness (Jung 1959, CW 9/1, § 290). Someone suffering from physical ailments may, for example, be asked to travel to the site of the symptom in the body in their mind's eye in order to explore emerging inner images. In this context, Verena Kast described a man who was complaining about a stiff neck, from which he had been suffering for six months. Two images emerged on his inner journey: He saw the yoke of an ox, then himself, as an artist in a circus arena, bearing a pole on his shoulders and neck. On this pole, he was balancing a chair into which a man jumped (Kast 2016, 169f). This image was in line with his personal perception, as he was carrying the weight of his company and his family on his shoulders, and both expected him to continue to function normally. With the help of imagination, he finally came up with a creative solution to getting rid of the pole and literally finding relief. At the end of the short exercise, he was able to move his head much more freely.

Getting in touch with one's body is also possible with Active Imagination, a method described by Jung as follows:

> The point is that you start with any image, [...] Contemplate it and carefully observe how the picture begins to unfold or to change. Don't try to make it into something, just do nothing but observe what its spontaneous changes are. Any mental picture you contemplate in this way will sooner or later change through a spontaneous association [...] You must carefully avoid impatient jumping from one subject to another. [...] Note all these changes and eventually step into the picture yourself, and if it is a speaking figure at all then say what you have to say to that figure and listen to what he or she has to say. (Jung 1973, Letters Vol. I, 460)

Active Imagination was also helpful for a 50-year-old lawyer suffering from Crohn's disease. In an initial brief image, he envisioned a vise attached to the right side of his abdomen, with the two jaws clamping his belly tightly like a workpiece, which was extremely painful. During the process of imagination, he met a ragged man who turned out to be the only person with the power to tighten or loosen the vise. By entering into a dialogue with this neglected aspect of his masculinity, the patient realized that he had been suppressing a strong feeling of homesickness in order to ensure his livelihood in a new country as quickly as possible. Accessing feelings of loss and grief made him increasingly aware of the connection between his psychological moods and physical symptoms. This not only reduced his feelings of powerlessness and helplessness, but also allowed him to engage in a new kind of self-care. By confronting the ragged man and his views in earnest, the lawyer's relationship to his body changed (for details on the indication, method, and limit of Active Imagination, see Dorst & Vogel 2014).

Imagination or mental imagery is not only important for patients, but also for therapists, especially in difficult treatment processes: During one session of therapy when Sue Austin was treating a woman so mired in self-hatred (Austin 2016a, 38) that the patient's rage erupted violently, Austin reacted not only by feeling disgusted, but also crushed, on the verge of tears and close to exploding herself. She was starting to hate the patient for her state of mind, but decided to remain silent, until suddenly a strong inner image emerged of the patient grabbing her by the neck, forcing her to kneel on the concrete floor and demanding that she eat the feces lying there. The therapist refused, as this was something she simply would not stoop to do. This mental image awakened a deep sense of shame in her because she struggled with the idea of allowing herself to eat like an animal. Still, she decided not to interpret these inner images, fearing that in doing so, she would ward them off and lose contact with these unbearably difficult emotions.

This coincides with Jung's reference to the dangers of understanding during the later stages of treatment: the Latin and Greek verbs for *understanding*, namely *comprehendere* and *katasullambanein*, respectively, allude to this fact with their basic meaning of *devouring* and *swallowing*. Jung held that the core of an individual is a mystery that may be eradicated once it is comprehended. Interpretative understanding, then, can be tantamount to the assassination of the soul, if vital differences are evened out. He rather advocates that individuals should make inroads towards hidden and not fully comprehensible symbols that harbor the seed of personality. This seed must not be spoken about and is the source of healing: "True understanding seems to be one which does not understand, yet lives and works" (Adler, Gerhard and Jaffé, Aniela, eds., *C.G. Jung: Letters*, Vol. 1, page 460). Jung therefore considers misunderstandings and disagreements between therapist and patient to be necessary phenomena in the developmental process as soon as the existential layers of personality are touched upon.

Imagination and phantasy bring us into contact with our playful side, something that people and animals the world over cultivate and cherish, and which, according to Winnicott, is essential to our health (Winnicott 1997, 51f), not least because playful imagination is a creative process (Jung 1971, CW 6, § 93). Play can open up a realm of possibility which acts as a counterpoint to overly rigid thoughts or behavior patterns. It was precisely this realm of playfulness that Austin was seeking to increase for her patient before beginning to address her despair (Austin 2016a, 28). From the perspective of Analytical Psychology, play has an archetypal quality in that it belongs to the collective heritage of humankind, as confirmed by neurobiologist Jaak Panksepp's research on the so-called PLAY system (Panksepp & Biven 2012, 453). When a therapist feels helpless or is confronted by something dreadful, imaginative play, movement, or exploration of potential spaces can be of (vital) importance, as well as encouraging patients themselves to venture into new realms of creation. Jung emphasizes that it is often not just a matter of wanting to play, but of having to play. Play is a serious activity because it derives from an inner compulsion. Anything new, and thus creative, does not emanate from the intellect, but from the playful, creative spirit (Jung 1971, CW 6, § 93 and 197).

1.4.3 Wishing, Hoping and Believing

In the process of imagination, the soul comes into contact with wishes, desires, fears, and creative possibilities, and things that we actually thought were impossible can become possible (Kast 2016, 11). People already heeded this long ago, as reflected in old sayings and fairytales, for example, "Faith can move mountains" or "In the days when wishing still helped." Those who ridicule these ideas should remember that even in the most enlightened people, an omnipresent readiness to experience a miracle often slumbers just below the surface, and according to Jung, those who most resist it are the first to become subject to its suggestive power (Jung 1969, CW 8, § 848). Admittedly, the potential impact of faith is not compelling, albeit already proven by science. There is no guarantee, and whether something actually manifests when we believe in, wish or hope for it remains uncertain. What is more, our ego cannot willfully select and attach these emotions to something specific, as this is decided by the unconscious. Wishing can probably only be effective if it is of an existential nature, originating in an archetypal layer of the soul, and if contact with what used to be called divine power has been established (Jung 1969, CW 8, § 957). This is what people seek when going on a pilgrimage to places of grace, such as Lourdes, to touch relics, and pray there to be healed. The increasingly widespread hope for so-called quantum healing should also be mentioned in this context. When people become fascinated, are shocked, or feel deeply moved in the process, then a massive shift towards the unconscious takes place and archetypes are stimulated, which may well include the archetype of healing (Jung 1969, CW 8, § 902). Things can occur which one person alone could never have hoped to bring about. Psychologically speaking, the unconscious is that extra something which transcends ego power and makes physical effects possible. Holocaust survivor Viktor Frankl was able to observe this under the extreme conditions in the concentration camp. He witnessed how physical survival depended less on physical strength and vitality than on the ability to find meaning in suffering, leaving him deeply impressed by the powerful effect of thought on the physical realm (Whitmont 1993, 31). This phenomenon was also addressed in a six-year study at the University of Iowa: A total of 557 men and women with an average age of 71 had the level of the inflammatory marker interleukin-6 determined in their blood. The subjects were included in the study because all of them were churchgoers, and it turned out that the most frequent churchgoers had the lowest level of inflammation. The mortality rate was also found to correlate with the frequency of church visits (Schubert/Amberger 2019, 130). Although church attendance cannot be equated with religiosity, one can probably assume that it is at least a contributing factor. If this were true, the study would be an indication that being connected to the Divine, participating in rituals, and belonging to a community of faith all promote physical health.

Considering the above, it is not surprising that a faithful, optimistic attitude tends to generate positive therapy results, whereas skepticism or resistance often have the opposite effect (Jung 1969, CW 8, § 970). This might also explain why the German chemist Max von Pettenkofer did not contract cholera, even though he voluntarily swallowed a live culture of cholera bacteria to disprove Robert Koch's claim that bacteria can cause disease. Pettenkofer was deeply convinced that these bacteria could not harm him.

The power that faith can have was also observed by Jewish writer Jean Améry, who was imprisoned and tortured in concentration camps for two years. He afterwards recounted an event which was totally unexpected for him: in the face of inhuman suffering, the intellectual world on which he had based his life and which he had relied on turned into something totally unreal. His conscious mind could not grapple with this realization and his intellectual interest, as well as that of other like-minded thinkers, gave way to a state of complete indifference. Having faith was different, and Améry, who called himself an intellectual agnostic, was able to observe that genuine believers possessed something indestructible that carried them through all misery (Jaffé 1984, 110).

But what happens when people's convictions do not coincide? What if beliefs differ strongly with regard to the interplay of body and soul, healing possibilities, or healing methods? In such cases, it would be helpful if everyone concerned, i.e., scientists, therapists, doctors, or laypersons, would admit, as a first step, that they have certain fundamental assumptions about the world on the basis of which they seek the truth about this reciprocity of body and soul. Depending on their personality and their present conscious and unconscious collective images, humans follow different paths to arrive at different models of reality, the relevance of which will be put forward in the next chapter.

2

Mind-Body Theories and their Relevance for Everyday Life and Therapy

2.1 Separation of Body and Psyche: Dualism

Jung begged to consider that in his day and age, the scientific methods available were too scanty to allow for a more detailed exploration of the nature of psyche and physis. However, based on his practical psychotherapeutic work, he considered it highly probable,

> ...that the psychic and the physical are not two independent parallel processes, but are essentially connected through reciprocal action, although the actual nature of this relationship is still completely outside our experience. (Jung 1969, CW 8, § 33)

In contrast to Jung's concept of the mind-body connection, the idea of an independent coexistence of psyche and body had gained increasing support by the beginning of the 16th century. René Descartes (1596-1650) is considered the most important representative of this physio-psychic dualism that viewed humans as consisting of two separate entities, body and soul. In his work "De homine" (1632), he describes the body as a machine which should be treated in the same way as clocks, mills, or similar mechanisms. He held that the human organism functions like a mechanical clock and once the technical processes have been understood, the cause-effect chains of diseases can then be investigated and treated accordingly. The soul is not needed for an understanding of bodily functions, so that describing and comprehending the physics of life (Schipperges 1999, 98) will suffice. The scientific knowledge of blood circulation, the structure of internal organs or the musculoskeletal system gained during Descartes' lifetime support this worldview. From then on, many physicians and anatomists understood the bodily realm as mechanistic, even if individual processes could not yet be totally grasped. As a matter of fact, humanity should be thankful for this dualistic worldview of medicine, as technical advancements in acute, intensive or transplant medicine, in artificial nutrition, dialysis, resuscitation and much more, frequently of a life-saving nature, would scarcely have been possible had the body not been regarded as a machine. According to Wolfgang Albert, physician and psychologist at the German Heart Center in Berlin, this mechanistic view is still widespread today. Numerous heart patients initially perceive their heart as a mechanical pump (Geisenhanslüke 2019, 163), and are admitted to hospital with the idea that their malfunctioning organ can be repaired through surgery or medication. Yet, as soon as they are scheduled for a heart transplant, men are less keen to receive a woman's heart, expressing preference for the heart of a man. It is at this point at the latest that it becomes obvious that a new heart is not viewed simply as a machine or a spare part, but evidently carries an emotional and symbolic meaning which can have an effect on the body. For example, when we speak of a "broken heart", the term is used not merely as a metaphor paraphrasing a grieve-stricken soul, but sometimes to describe a physical correlate. Deep sorrow or other emotional stressors have been known to not only burden the soul, but can also lead to physical damage of the heart with chest pain, pulmonary edema, and severe left ventricular dysfunction (Malarkey et al. 2015, 44). This "broken heart syndrome" can occasionally be fatal and shows how closely connected our emotions are to the body.

Within this context, the simplistic machine model has reached its limitations and is rather inappropriate. When it comes to chronic illnesses, the dualistic paradigm frequently ends in disaster, with patients no longer adequately diagnosed, let alone treated, if isolated from their psyche, subjectivity, social environment, or relationships (Schubert 2015a, IX). Even though the mutual influence of psyche and body has been proven in the field of psychosomatics today, Schubert holds that this happens in a mostly deep-rooted dualistic mode of thinking. To my mind, what we experience in our daily lives hardly allows us to shake off such a dualistic world-view. An image that comes to mind would be the soul living in the body, as illustrated in the Jewish encyclopedia "Sepher Haolamoth". Here, the human body is likened to a house in which the soul lives, i.e., an ensouled temple (Meier 1979, 54). In Jungian Psychology, the body as matter (derived from the Latin mater = mother) is a term that already expresses the idea of the Great Mother – body and earth are practically synonymous. Physical problems can therefore be understood as being problems with the mother archetype.

The spirit as the opposite pole belongs to the father archetype (von Franz 1992, 16) opening up a field of tension and relations between two fundamental opposites. This polarity or duality between female-male or mother and father is a widespread concept found in many schools of thought or phenomena. In the Hebrew language, for example, only consonants are written down, whereas vowels have to be recognized and filled in automatically by the speaker. Vowels are provided by the male spirit, consonants by the female body, i.e., by everything that appears in the physical realm (Weinreb 1985, 16).

Even in today's information age, there exist dualistic views of the mind-body relationship, with the body being described as hardware and the psyche as the corresponding software. Such imagery raises interesting questions: Can my hardware be exchanged, that is, my psyche be transferred to another set of hardware? And could physical death be outwitted to allow my psyche to live on in another form? Philosopher Luciano Floridi seeks answers to these questions by providing analogies: "Indeed, there can be no butterfly without the caterpillar, but once the butterfly is born, the caterpillar is no longer needed for the butterfly to live."

Today's information culture therefore seems to embrace the idea that a body is necessary to allow for the birth of a personality, consciousness, mind, and soul, but once all of this has emerged from the physical realm, the existence of the initial body is no longer required. This does not mean the psyche can do away with a physical platform altogether, but perhaps there are other mediums, similarly well suited to this task (Floridi 2015, 99f). This would only be possible, however, if body and soul could exist independently of each other.

Looking at the research results of neurobiologist Antonio Damasio, mind and consciousness do not appear to be transferable. He distinguishes between the conscious content localized in the cortical brain structures and the state of consciousness. According to his findings, the latter arises in the brain stem, namely through information which ascends from the inner body. It is a form of representation, reflecting a person's momentary visceral condition: This is who I am, and this is how I feel right now. Consciousness equals feeling what is going on in the body at a given moment, which to Damasio would be unthinkable without a body (Damasio 2000, 26).

Jung had already grasped this connection intuitively when describing the emotion rooted in the body as the main source of emerging awareness (Jung 1959, CW 9/1, § 179) – an idea also reflected in language: the Greek word *menin* means not only *anger*, but is also the root of the English term *mind*. Anger would thus be a source of both spirit and mind.

2.2 Only One of the Two Exists: Monistic Materialism and Monistic Idealism

Rather than pursuing dualism, most neuroscientists today adhere to a so-called monistic-materialistic viewpoint, which holds that everything emerges from underlying matter. This model assumes that mental life is the metabolic product of a huge cluster of neurons, so that suffering, feelings, consciousness, goals, or one's own identity are all in fact the result of neuronal activity. Everything mental is the result of underlying physical processes, as propagated by some German book titles.[1] The physical realm is primary and gives rise to soulful and spiritual experiences.

This idea is not entirely new. Back in the 19th century, psychologist William James and pathologist Carl Georg Lange developed their Theory of Emotion, holding that people do

1. For example: *Bauplan für eine Seele* (Blueprint for a Soul) by Dietrich Dörner, or *Wie das Gehirn die Seele macht* (How the Brain Creates the Soul) by Gerhardt Roth & Nicole Strüber.

not cry because they are sad, but conversely are sad because they cry, angry because they strike a blow, and frightened because they tremble. James' hypothesis is that the states of consciousness emerging from emotions such as grief, fear, anger, or love are the result of bodily phenomena. Researchers such as Darwin and Pavlov, as well as the school of Behaviorism also favor this concept, in which the psyche is seen as a by-product of physical circuits (Meier 1994, 223f).

Even though neurobiologists have been able to identify brain regions that correlate with various perceptions, feelings, thoughts, and conscious phenomena, their localization is far from explaining how mind, consciousness and soul are supposed to emerge from matter. To this day, researchers and especially supporters of the materialistic-monistic position have not been able to find out how exactly this leap from the physical substrate to the spirit and soul is brought about.

Jung was no friend of the materialistic attitude which understands the psyche as a kind of secretion of the brain, comparable to bile as a product of the liver:

> The psyche deserves to be taken as a phenomenon in its own right; there are no grounds at all for regarding it as a mere epiphenomenon, dependent though it may be on the functioning of the brain. One would be as little justified in regarding life as an epiphenomenon of the chemistry of carbon compounds. (Jung 1969, CW 8, § 10)

This does not offer proof, but is rather an assessment, in which he emphasizes his view that the psyche deserves to be regarded as an autonomous entity. A psychotherapist with a high esteem for the psychic realm will not be surprised by this attitude or even doubt it. A materialist will demand evidence for such a view, because a mental or spiritual existence independent of a body has yet to be confirmed: "*How, exactly, does a thought (which has no physical properties whatsoever) cause the physical stuff of neurons to start firing? This violates all the known laws of physics*" (Solms & Turnbull 2003, 53). Even Jung could not fathom in which way an immaterial psyche could ever bring about anything material, but conversely, also wondered how chemical processes could ever produce mental ones (Jung 1969, CW 8, § 938).

For followers of monistic idealism, these are non-questions, as they consider the spirit to be the only thing that exists and from which everything emanates, including matter. The Celts already understood matter as the realization of thoughts or imagination, a worldview shared by surgeon Richard Selzer who writes that "*the body is the spirit thickened*" (Morris 1991, 262). Similarly, Ludwig Wittgenstein declares that "*the human body is the best image of the human soul.*" The body would thus be an aggregate state of the spirit, which the behavior of water may serve to illustrate. Depending on the environmental conditions, water appears in vaporous, liquid, or solid form. Were we not in a position to observe the phases of transition between these different aggregate states, or were we ignorant of the chemical formula for water, we would hardly assume that its different physical conditions were based on one and the same substance. In his "It-from-bit" hypothesis, American physicist John Archibald Wheeler also explains that every entity in the material world is based on something immaterial, meaning that matter is of informational origin and psyche and body should be regarded as distinct informational states (Floridi 2015, 100). In the East, some Tantrists cultivated a similar idea, namely that matter is nothing but the determinacy of God's thoughts (von Franz 1992, 16) – an empirically unverifiable notion and rather close to the ideas of monistic idealism.

2.3 A Mysterious Primordial Substance: Dual Aspect Monism

Everyday human experience clearly reflects the dualistic notion of having a body that serves as a vessel for the soul and the spirit. People are well aware that without a body, there would be no feelings, thoughts or laughter. For as soon as this body vessel breaks, it is not only the physical form that dies, but psychic life as we know it. The human psyche and body cannot exist separately from each other, and in this respect, are companions in fate. In a mysterious way, they are perhaps even a unity, that is, an indivisible whole.

Back in 1929, natural scientist Bertrand Russell mentioned in this context that "I am of the opinion that matter is less material, and mind is less spiritual than commonly assumed" (quoted in Meier 1975, 10). Similarly, Marie-Louise von Franz presumed that "in the deepest layers of the collective unconscious, we approach something unobservable that cannot be distinguished from matter" (von Franz 1992, 207). Both of them thus assume that the conventional separation of physics and psychology, of mind and matter, is untenable.

This kind of separation is also rejected by the two neuropsychologists Mark Solms and Oliver Turnbull, supporters of the so-called dual-aspect monism, which postulates that "we are made of only one type of stuff, but we perceive this stuff in two different ways" (Solms & Turnbull 2003, 56), and that human nature is neither mental nor physical. In Solms' and Turnbull's view, the brain is made of something that appears to be physical when viewed from the outside as an object, and mental when viewed from the inside. Perceiving ourselves externally in a mirror and internally through introspection means observing the same entity in two different ways: as a body and a psychic being. In this mind-body model, the difference between body, mind and spirit would then be a mere artifact of perception and we would never be able to perceive the "stuff" we are made of. In principle, it would be impossible to apprehend the two sides of one and the same identity in a holistic and simultaneous manner – which is probably why we cannot avoid using dualistic language when describing mind-body phenomena. Psychoneuroimmunologist Broom also assumes that the mysterious leap from the psychic to the physical realm may be a perceptual artifact: "*The mysterious is mysterious only because there is no such 'leap' at all [...] There is no leap from the psychic realm to the brain and no leap from the brain to the body. The 'leap' is a concept derived from human categorizations*" (*translated from the German original*) (Broom 2015, 375).

These ideas are consistent with the following statements by Jung:

> Since psyche and matter are contained in one and the same world, and moreover are in continuous contact with one another and ultimately rest on irrepresentable, transcendental factors, it is not only possible but fairly probable, even, that psyche and matter are two different aspects of one and the same thing. (Jung 1969, CW 8, § 418)

and

> Mind and body are presumably a pair of opposites and, as such, the expression of a single entity whose essential nature is not knowable either from its outward, material manifestation or from inner, direct perception. [...] This living being appears outwardly as the material body, but inwardly as a series of images of the vital

> activities taking place within it. They are two sides of the same coin, and we cannot rid ourselves of the doubt that perhaps this whole separation of mind and body may finally prove to be merely a device of reason for the purpose of conscious discrimination – an intellectually necessary separation of one and the same fact into two aspects. (Jung 1969, CW 8, § 619)

and

> The distinction between mind and body is an artificial dichotomy, an act of discrimination based far more on the peculiarity of intellectual cognition than on the nature of things. (Jung 1971, CW 6, § 916)

Von Franz also tends to recognize matter and mind as one and the same reality, which can be described by physics and depth psychology in a complementary manner when viewed from the outside or inside. The introspectively perceivable collective unconscious is recognized as a material reality by atomic physics (von Franz 1992, 40 and 169).

Jung thus understands the unwarranted separation of mind and body as a consequence of human awareness. It is the ability to perceive opposites or polarities. Mind and body have thus become a pair of opposites, with the former showing itself internally as the dynamic, moving, and inspiring aspect, while the latter is visible on the outside in the form of instincts, physiology, and sensual perception (Jung 1969, CW 8, § 619). As soon as we become conscious, we cannot avoid perceiving mind and matter separately.

The idea of dual aspect monism was also shared by Jewish scholar Friedrich Weinreb, who saw humans as an imperceptible unity in which the body and spirit oppose each other as a paradox (Weinreb 1999, 11). He sees the Bible as a collective human dream with symbolic descriptions of the world. As for the mind-body problem, Weinreb refers to the second chapter of Genesis which illustrates the creation of humankind: God created the first man from clay and brought him into the Garden of Eden, where he was put into a deep sleep. In a second step, God then took one of the two sides of the man's body (not just the rib, as claimed by the translation) to create a woman. Initially, a human being was thus an undivided whole, only split into male and female in the second step. While the male half represents the inner world, the soul, the female half symbolizes the flesh, the physical-material life, the physical realm. This symbolism applies to men and women as well as all living beings in that the body is the symbolic feminine and the spirit is the symbolic masculine. Their separation by the conscious mind is the requirement for their relationship to come into being, an idea shared by analyst Susan Bach, who understood psyche and soma as the world's oldest married couple. This relationship can be amicable and loving, seeing them walking harmoniously hand in hand in good times, often without even being aware of their respective other part (Bach 1990, 120). But it may also be characterized by dislike, hatred, fear, or even war during trying times.

The phenomenon of the dual aspect of one and the same thing is not that exceptional and known, e.g., in the context of light. Over the past hundred years, physicists have had to describe light as a corpuscle in one instance, and as a wave in another. Light presents itself with two different faces, which can never be observed simultaneously. Depending on the experiment, light can emerge as a wave or a particle, and physicists have to accept this as a fact. By analogy, body and soul can be perceived by humans as two incompatible sides of one and the same phenomenon, in the same way that gravity is proof that non-observable phenomena exist. Indeed, no one doubts their existence, although we lack proof thereof and can merely perceive their effects.

Drawing on medieval natural philosophy, Jung used the term "Unus mundus" (which literally translates to *the one world underlying everything*) to refer to a potential, unified reality of psyche and matter behind this dualistic view, which could serve as a background to the empirical world (Jung 1963, CW 14/2, § 414).

A glance at the history books shows that the idea of a "Unus mundus" has a long tradition among philosophers, theologians, and physicians. Paracelsus (1493-1541) was also convinced of a primordial entity or substance which preceded the separation of the physical and the spiritual (Maio 2012, 104). He therefore recommended that a person's external nature be observed conscientiously as this makes the internal nature visible, as a reflection of the exterior. According to ancient Egyptian belief, the "Unus mundus" is only attainable after death as a holistic experience, in which spirit, mind and body merge into one (von Franz 1992, 57). At an unconscious level, such a notion could sustain the Catholic belief that resurrection after death relates to not only the mind, but also to the body.

The archaic German word *Leib* (= *body*) is rarely used today. Similar to the Middle High German word *lip*, it means *life*, still evidenced by some German expressions like "bei*leib*e nicht" (= by no means), which actually means "by no *life*". The term *liver* also belongs to the concept of body and life, and it was in fact regarded as the seat of the vital juices in ancient times. Is there a difference between the German word *Körper* (= body), more commonly used today, and its archaic form? *Körper* is derived from the Latin word *corpus*, on which English terms like the archaic *corse* or *corpse* are based. Body, mortality, death, and decay are thus closely related in many languages. The German term for corpse is *Leichnam*, whose literal meaning is *clothing of the body* – an inanimate shell, a mere exterior of existence (Küchenhoff & Wiegerling 2008, 9).

In Jewish tradition, what we would call *Leib* in German consists of the same organs, limbs, and functions as the German *Körper*.[2] But *Leib* contains the certainty that whatever happens to the *Körper*, something will still persist – there is something that always was, always is and always will be. It thus reaches beyond earthly life and into eternity. *Leib* breaks through the limitations of the word *Körper*, inviting humans to recognize themselves as eternal beings. In this respect, the concept of *Leib* refers to, or could even be a designation for, the "Unus mundus." *Körper* would thus be a *Leib* in its temporal aspect and in its concrete appearance, with the former merely being a part of the latter (Weinreb 1987, 12, 20). Critics will say that such a construct may be believed or not – and so be it.

A holistic reality, or holistic experience, in which everything is connected similar to a "Unus mundus", is experienced by some people during clinical death. These so-called near-death experiences were scientifically investigated in a prospective Dutch study on near-death experiences during cardiac arrest. It was conducted by cardiologist Pim van Lommel (van Lommel 2011), who followed affected patients for up to eight years after their near-death experience, recording medical/physical findings, psychological experiences during clinical death, and enquiring about any ensuing personality changes.

During near-death experiences, people can have out-of-body experiences that can be readily verified after the event. Some describe leaving their body behind without losing their

2. *Translator's note*: As mentioned, the German word *Leib* is the archaic form of the German *Körper* and no longer in common use, although still present in some dated terms and expressions (Leibarzt (personal doctor), Leibgericht (favourite dish). Both terms (*Leib* and *Körper*) translate as *body* in English.

identity or personal consciousness. Instead of residing in their old material body, they possess a kind of immaterial body from which they can observe their material body and everything that happens to it from above. In this state of disembodiment, they observe details that according to current knowledge, unconscious patients can actually neither see nor hear. When they wake up and recount these details, nurses and doctors are amazed at the correctness and accuracy of the events described by their patients. A medically well-documented near-death experience is available from Pamela Reynolds, whose brain metabolism stopped near the brain stem for an hour during surgery. Her body was cooled down to 10 degrees Celsius and she was connected to a heart-lung machine. Despite meeting brain death criteria, she had an out-of-body experience, could hear the doctors' conversations, and moved towards a light which she understood to be the breath of God (van Lommel 2014, 184ff).

Based on his own and other study results, van Lommel designed the model of Endless Consciousness which is bound neither to a specific time nor place. Such non-local consciousness has no beginning or end and is constantly present around us and within us. It is also timeless, for in this state of being, past, present, and future exist at the same time.

In this model, the brain acts as a receiving station for the Endless Consciousness, of which, however, it can only receive a fraction. Van Lommel compares the function of the brain with a television set, which translates omnipresent invisible electromagnetic fields into pictures and sounds. But the brain is not only a receiver, it is also a transmitter, broadcasting information from the inside of the body and the individual psyche to the Endless Consciousness. In this model, the brain does not exhibit a creative function – as neuroscientists or materialists would describe it today – but acts merely as a facilitator and transmitter. As a resonance organ for the Endless Consciousness, it facilitates individual experiences of consciousness. Van Lommel is not the only supporter of this concept, with neuroscientists such as John Eccles, Wilder Penfield or Charles Sherrington in alignment with his view (van Lommel 2014, 219).

Van Lommel knows that his idea of Endless Consciousness can neither be demonstrated nor measured on a scientific basis (van Lommel 2014, 22), but interestingly enough, it largely coincides with Jung's concept of the collective unconscious:

> For in the unconscious psyche space and time seem to be relative; that is to say, knowledge finds itself in a space-time continuum in which space is no longer space, nor time time. (Jung 1969, CW 8, § 912)

Near-death experiences are very similar in terms of the sequence of events, and thus, not very individual. People at all times and in all cultures generally describe the same contents (van Lommel 2014, 149), which also corresponds to the idea of a collective unconscious, effective as a non-personal part of the unconscious in all people, times and cultures. What is more, the difference between good and evil, i.e., the oppositional tension of consciousness, is no longer present in people's accounts of near-death experiences, reflecting yet another characteristic of Jung's description of the collective unconscious.

The near-death experience of one of his patients also led Jung to ponder about intense experiences during states of unconsciousness, when according to human knowledge, neither conscious activities nor sensual perceptions are possible (Jung 1969, CW 8, § 937). His patient had lost a lot of blood during a complicated forceps delivery and subsequently, lost consciousness for half an hour. After waking up, she reported very typical near-death experiences, namely how from above, she had watched the worried doctor fighting for her life. But she also recounted a journey to a gateway into another, colorful and joyful world, which is common in such experiences, as well as the knowledge that had she crossed this threshold, a return to life would have been impossible.

Jung's reflections about a consciousness that might possibly detach itself from the body or the brain in such near-death experiences, and about the idea of a psyche connected to a living brain that should therefore be dispensed with (Jung 1969, CW 8, § 937), resemble van Lommel's idea of an Endless Consciousness independent of the body. In this context, the seemingly crazy concept of philosopher Floridi regarding a possible transfer of the individual psyche to another carrier, also appears in a new light (see Chapter 2.1, Separation of Body and Psyche: Dualism), as does the hope of some people to be able to "save" their spirit and keep it alive beyond the death of their physical body.

Paradoxically, near-death experiences revert us to the concept of dualism, because these are not only holistic experiences, but connected to a leaving of the material body, which is observed from the outside. The mind-body problem thus remains mysterious.

In the context of near-death experiences, Jung discussed whether consciousness could not only be localized in the brain, as usually assumed, but also in the sympathetic nervous system – an idea based on bee research carried out at the time. It had in fact been assumed that insects were only capable of reflex-like behavior because of their ventral nerve cord. However, Karl von Frisch's bee research had subsequently shown that bees not only communicate to their hive mates that they have located a feeding place, but also in which direction and at what distance food can be found. Such an exchange of information could never occur on an unconscious level among humans, but only in the form of conscious communication. Thus, the ventral nerve cord appears to be astonishingly efficient with regard to perception and complex communication, which is why the human sympathetic nervous system cannot be ruled out as a possible carrier of psychic functions during states of unconsciousness (Jung 1969, CW 8, § 946f).

Van Lommel also searched for biological causes to near-death experiences, namely in the protein dimethyltriptamine (DMT), produced by the pineal gland (epiphysis). During episodes of intense physical stress, such as a heart attack, the body releases large amounts of the stress hormones cortisol, adrenaline, and noradrenaline, which in turn stimulate the production of DMT. When administered intravenously, it is known to cause experiences that bear a striking resemblance to near-death experiences, such as the feeling of being outside one's body, encounters with light beings or the feeling of unconditional love. Van Lommel therefore suggests that DMT removes the natural blockage in the body, which prevents such experiences in everyday life (van Lommel 2014, 134).

2.4 C.G. Jung's Concept of Synchronicity

Around 1200 BC, based on the hypothesis of the unity of all Being in nature, the Chinese King Wen and his Duke Dschou explored the connection between mental and physical states. They assumed that the same Being would show itself simultaneously in the psyche and the physis, and that matter and psyche would be reflections of a single Being. In order to grasp this coincidence of the inner (unconscious) and outer (physical) states, a special method was used in which yarrow stalks were thrown six times in a row. Nowadays, these have been mostly replaced by three coins, and depending on whether they come up heads or tails, three or two points are awarded, resulting in a total of six numbers between six and nine. Even numbers are assigned to the female principle yin, and odd numbers to the male principle yang.

With this throwing method, a total of 64 yin-yang number combinations are possible, which are documented in the Chinese wisdom book *I Ching*, still used today. The idea is to render the quality of any given moment conscious and understandable, which Chinese scholars achieved by translating all number combinations into linguistic images and metaphors, so that the meaning of a situation was intuitively interpreted. It can therefore be regarded as a mantic method with indications of future tendencies. The required coin tossing to capture the meaning of a certain moment in time is not a causal process, but an irrational method and an example of synchronicity as defined by C.G. Jung.

It was only after years of hesitation that Jung ventured to publish his concept of synchronicity in 1952, not least because a few decades earlier, quantum physics and the relativity theory had shaken the previously valid understanding of nature. The principle of causality applied in macrophysics and thus, the connection between cause and effect, was not practical in physics based on the smallest particles of matter. In a complementary manner, Jung therefore contrasted the principle of causality with that of synchronicity as a causeless state of arrangement. Synchronicity is the coincidence of an inner-mental and one or more outer-material phenomena, whereby this concurrence does not appear to be a trivial, but a meaningful event for those involved (Jung 1969, CW 8, § 843). Making sense of or attaching meaning to something entails human judgement, and what makes sense to one person may be perceived as nonsense, absurdity, or pointlessness by another because of its subjective, holistic nature. When inner and outer events come to coincide, we experience a sense of meaning or purpose. Sinologist Richard William translated the term *Tao* in this way to denote an Eastern philosophy that assumes an objective, global meaning with an a priori existence in the collective unconscious, the very place where opposites are not yet separated. As soon as yes and no, light and dark, right and wrong are identified, meaning fades and becomes less and less easily recognizable (Jung 1969, CW 8, § 913). This original world meaning has no cause, but is simply a given, similar to a living body, in which different parts function in a synchronistic manner in accordance with each other. In the same way, global events are interrelated with no underlying cause – they simply occur as an arrangement of Being.

Jung therefore deliberated the question whether near-death experiences could be synchronistic phenomena, as they lack any causal connection with physiological processes. The very nature of synchronistic phenomena is that they are independent of time and space and, by definition, not based on sensual perceptions – all of which would meet the criteria of Jung's definition (Jung 1969, CW 8, § 955).

Hence, a synchronistic event always consists of two factors, namely "an unconscious idea which comes into consciousness in the form of a dream, idea, or premonition, and an objective situation which coincides with the content" (Jung 1969, CW 8, § 858). When looking at synchronicity, it is therefore important to identify any arrangement and pattern of events whose causes cannot be explained. Experience shows that the probability of impressive synchronistic events increases with the intensity of affects. The more emotionally charged a situation, the more frequently spectacular individual cases of synchronicity will occur. Jung mentions the example of two sisters in England who had counted heavily on inheriting an old mansion with landed property. However, a distant cousin was given the estate instead. Filled with hatred, they were sitting before their open fireplace, when one of them suggested painting a picture of the heir and throwing it into the fire. That same night, the mansion burned down (Jung 1961, 3). In this particular case, Jung ruled out any causal relationship, for it was not apparent how their burning the effigy could result in setting on fire the house which was a great distance away, any more than the fire could have sparked the sisters' fantasy. He therefore sees the two events as synchronistic occurrences, i.e., the usually hidden order of Being is revealed in a psychic and external process. Jung is aware that many people are reluctant to accept such an interpretation and would rather refer to a trivial coincidence or prefer to adopt a causal perspective, assuming that some kind of transmission has taken place. In a spectacular case such as the above, magic is the term that often comes to mind, but Jung rejects the notion of magical causality and instead resorts to the concept of synchronicity, which is based on a meaningful correspondence of natural events (Jung 1969, CW 8, § 905). In a less spectacular fashion, psychiatrist Jan Kalbitzer (Kalbitzer 2018, 33) relates how a seagull pooped on his head, completely ruining his coat, after he had once again interfered in his wife's daily life by criticizing her over the phone. Others would have considered this a trivial coincidence, but this synchronistic event made sense to him, since he interpreted it as a hint to abandon his know-it-all attitude. In another example, a woman had a similar impression, when one morning, completely out of the blue, she "sensed death around her" – which made her cry and very sad, although she was certain that it was not a premonition of her own death. A few hours later, she received the news that her father, who lived many thousand miles away, had died at around that time. Again, Jung would not speak of magical transmission in this case, but of synchronicity, because the information present in the collective unconscious can be perceived by the ego, especially in emotionally highly charged situations.

If one, like Jung, understands this *being arranged* as an ever-present natural principle - comparable to the Tao - then not only can such spectacular one-time events as those experienced by the two sisters be expected, but an ongoing psychophysical mirroring, similar to the "pre-stabilized harmony", as formulated by Wilhelm Leibniz (Jung 1969, CW 8, § 927). Jung therefore pondered whether the relationship of body and soul, the coordination of psychic and physical processes, should therefore also be understood as a synchronistic phenomenon:

> The synchronicity principle possesses properties that may help to clear up the body-soul problem. Above all, it is the fact of causeless order, or rather, of meaningful orderedness, that may throw light on psychophysical parallelism. (Jung 1969, CW 8, § 948)

and

> The synchronicity phenomena point, it seems to me, in this direction, for they show that the non-psychic can behave like the psychic, and vice versa, without there being any causal connection between them. (Jung 1969, CW 8, § 418)

and

> As far as we can discern, the collective unconscious is identical with nature [...] including matter. I could not object to the assumption that psyche is a quality of

> matter or that matter is the concrete aspect of psyche, provided that "psyche" were defined as the collective unconscious (*translated from the original*). (Jung 1961, 4)

The idea that something non-psychic can behave as if it were psychic and vice versa is also shared by Christian Schubert. He takes up Jung's idea of synchronicity in formulating that brain, psyche, and the immune system interact with each other in a psychosomatically synchronized manner by sharing a highly complex information network (Schubert 2015c, 106).

These propositions prepare the ground for an understanding of psychosomatics that focuses on the way the collective unconscious arranges both physis and psyche in the form of events which tend to happen simultaneously. Physis and psyche are two sides of the same coin, and physical and psychic symptoms can be considered symbolic images of an archetypal field. Unfathomable to humans, one or more archetypes in the collective unconscious are busy arranging our Being – including diseases. Psychosomatics from a Jungian point of view would move this arrangement into the center of reflection, exploring the activation of a particular archetypal field and the symbolic meaning of physical and psychic symptoms. In this context, physical and psychological symptoms are not always visible at the same time, for the body may speak out first, followed by the psyche, or vice versa. Yet, in addressing the symptom, that which was initially hidden usually becomes apparent, as implied in the origin of the Greek word *symptom. Symptosis* means the point of intersection between two curves, the confluence of two streams, the meeting of two, from which a third arises. This is what we refer to as a symptom, and this "third" can at the same time be regarded as a symbol (Meier 1994, 228f).

The collective unconscious is not only in charge of arranging disease or health, but also shapes the Zeitgeist and in turn, collective consciousness. At any given time, a society's current trends and values are indicative of the archetypal themes active in the collective unconscious. Recognizing socially relevant ideas or fields of conflict allows the prediction of developments to some extent, as despite their more modern appearance, questions relating to humanity will continue to transcend time. The concept of arrangement would see illnesses entering our lives seemingly without cause, which would be rather disturbing to many of us, because the inexplicable is always more difficult to bear than the explicable. People would feel at the mercy of this process, lacking control. Kalbitzer experienced such a situation when he lay down on his bed one day and, after closing his eyes, suddenly felt an intense emptiness pervade his body. His bed no longer seemed to provide any support and he felt himself plunging into dark depths. Retrospectively, no external causes could be identified, and he could re-evoke this extremely frightening state by simply closing his eyes (Kalbitzer 2018, 18) and embarking on external and internal journeys. He came to realize that, among other things, society was placing increasing demands on and exerting control over both his and other people's bodily needs, instincts, and emotions to the point that this played an important role in issues of health and illness (Kalbitzer 2018, 76).

Jung emphasized that neuroses are intimately linked with the problems of a particular era and its Zeitgeist, and thus regarded them as failed attempts by individuals to solve a universal problem within themselves – which in my opinion also applies to many psychosomatic or physical illnesses (Jung 1966, CW 7, § 18). Illness would thus be closely related to the spiritual guiding principles of an epoch, which appears to be commonly accepted. It seems plausible to many that psychiatric disorders, such as anorexia, burnout, or ADHD, are co-generated by societal values and demands. In this context, it would be worth exploring whether the surge in physical illnesses, such as allergies, autoimmune diseases, cancer, or dementia, could likewise allude to an archetypal theme in the collective unconscious. The more dominant an archetypal constellation is, the more people would fall ill. This complements a biological point of view that looks for physical causes or material environmental factors. The sick therefore suffer an illness which is representative of the whole of society and does not belong to or affect them as individuals only.

Such considerations complement the current notion of psychosomatics, which is predominantly inclined towards psychoanalytical concepts and favors a causal dependency of bodily symptoms on (individual) psychological factors or vice versa. This standpoint always sees the cause preceding the effect – a notion which is not fundamentally flawed, but probably incomplete. Viktor von Weizsäcker also expresses this view in arguing that by introducing the psyche into pathogenesis, the causal perspective has been relegated into a subordinate status (quoted from Meier 1994, 226).

2.5 Relevance of Mind-Body Theories for Psychotherapeutic Practice

Different mind-body models exist, but which one is "correct" and have we even touched upon it so far?

Psychosomatics not only examines the interaction between body and soul, but derives therapeutic concepts from it, so that considerations about the nature and relationship between the two are of fundamental importance. Solms and Turnbull "*are of the opinion that the nature of the relationship between brain and mind (body and soul) is not amenable to scientific proof*" (Solms & Turnbull 2003, 55). As a consequence, the process by which matter dissolves into mind and soul, i.e., the age-old mind-body problem, would not be accessible to present-day science and would therefore remain a mystery. Everything that is mysterious and beyond present knowledge, though, can only be grasped in symbolic form, and until a scientific hypothesis is found to support a yet unknown fact, it remains a symbol (Jung 1971, CW 6, § 822). This is, in fact, the best possible designation for something that is relatively unknown. The inexpressible, incomprehensible, inconceivable – anything not clearly known and only conjectured at is represented as a symbol. If it appeals to or touches us emotionally, which also holds true for a theory, it might have an invigorating, often also healing effect in that it conveys a sense of security, which need not be conscious at all.

The body-soul hypothesis which appears most plausible on a personal level may not only carry people through life, but also influences – more or less consciously – their view of the world and the whole of humanity. Those who regard mind and soul as the result of bodily processes will often conclude that life ends with physical death and mental illnesses are to be treated primarily or even exclusively as metabolic disorders or physical inflammation. But those who think of body, mind and soul as interrelated phenomena or expressions of a mysterious "primordial substance" will not only enquire about the fate of the soul after death, but dismiss psychosomatic concepts that fail to embrace mental and unconscious phenomena.

If it is true – and there is indeed some evidence to support this – that people can "merely" believe in the various mind-body models, it becomes clear how difficult a dialogue or mutual understanding between people of different views on the topic can be.

Foreseeing such difficulties, Jung hesitated for years to publish his concept of synchronicity "in order not to expose himself to thoughtless ridicule" (Jung 1969, CW 8, § 816). Non-observance is another behavior found in this context: When physician and scientist Christian Schubert wanted a comment he had on an article about childhood asthma to be included in the renowned journal *Lancet* because it contained not a single mention or hint of the scientifically proven link between emotional stress and the later onset of the disease, the editors decided not to print his comment, but forwarded it directly to the authors instead, who showed little interest in pursuing a discussion (Schubert & Exenberger 2015, 127). Similarly, the physician Pim van Lommel was labeled as "a disturbed prophet with a premorbid quack personality" by a gynecologist in view of his studies on near-death experiences and his concept of Endless Consciousness.

Furthermore, a general practitioner added that "when scientists start spouting nonsense, someone has to make the public aware of this stuff of the devil or confidence trickery, and proclaim the patients and staff interviewed as disingenuous and untrustworthy" (van Lommel 2014, 166). The last accusation especially shows that explosive questions of faith seem to be at stake here. Analytical Psychology holds that complex issues are activated, tempting people to attack opposing views by devaluing, insulting, or defaming them, thus preventing almost any kind of open curiosity or constructive skepticism. The complex in question could relate to our worldview, whose coherence is at risk of being crushed by new ideas. In this context, coherence means an inherently consistent, harmonious worldview which we experience as providing support, identity and meaning. Every person has such basic assumptions about life, which serve as a starting point for human values, decisions, and actions. Most of the time, we look for like-minded people who share our worldview, so that we can protect ourselves from unpleasant doubts. If our worldviews and concepts of illness are in alignment, we will find ourselves in a common boat, closer to each other, more familiar and safer, as like-minded people provide support against anything that might destroy our conceptions.

Clashing worldviews, on the other hand, can be very painful in that a certain degree of dissonance and distance must be endured, and a display of true tolerance is needed. If this is not possible, disputes centering on the prerogative of interpretation might result in mutual reproaches, cocksuredness, or finger-pointing. What is being advocated here is not so much a strict belief in the "right" theory as the possibility of giving oneself and others space for one's own convictions and experiences, the more so as "*it is possible to find merit in all of these different philosophical positions. It is also possible, with a little effort, to make all of them look ridiculous*" (Solms & Turnbull 2003, 54).

When someone dear to us, or we ourselves fall seriously ill, we find ourselves confronted with our very own personal mind-body concept, as exemplified by the case of a woman whom I will call Irene:

Irene knew she did not have much longer to live. She was sure that once she died, life for her body would be over, as reflected by the materialistic-monistic hypothesis, and she regarded this end to her life as a wall behind which was a dark nothingness or an indescribable void. A great wave of fear welled up inside of her, she felt bitter about her brief life and hatred, anger, and envy towards those who were healthy and would outlive her. Relationships with people close to her became toxic, as she could scarcely bear their show of compassion and attention. When Irene was hospitalized shortly before her death, she shared a room with a bedridden old woman who was visited every day by her husband, who very patiently read stories to her all afternoon. This got on her nerves and irritated Irene increasingly to the point that she asked to be moved to another room, which turned out to be impossible. One evening, while the couple was praying together, she suddenly felt overcome by an inner peace the likes of which she had never felt before, and which gave her an inexplicable sense of support and security during the last weeks of her life. Finding an explanation or meaning was not the key factor here, but the experience itself and its meticulous observation – this was "religio" in the truest sense of the word. Irene would have liked to live on, but this wish was not granted to her.

The prerogative of interpretation can be a battle of wills and play a major role in doctor-patient relationships, as exemplified by the case of an anorexic woman. When she refused to eat her pasta claiming she did not like it, the nurse accused her of lying, saying it was not the taste that prevented her from eating, but the calories she did not want to put on. The nurse was probably correct in assuming that the patient's view of the world, in which a real aversion towards or disgust for food figured, was determined by reducing the number of calories she consumed. Psychotherapist Doris Lier therefore refuses to label the woman a liar or to embarrass her in any way, suggesting instead that the patient's description be accepted as true and coherent within the context of her worldview. To disregard such an approach would harbor the risk of both patient and therapist becoming set in their diametrically opposed worldviews, rendering further discussion impossible. It was therefore not surprising that the embarrassed patient ate up her food, but proceeded to vomit later on (Lier 2001,

61f). Without a doubt, the severely anorectic patient needed to eat, and the impotent rage of the nurse, who initially failed to motivate her into doing so, is quite understandable. Yet, devaluating a patient's worldview in therapy out of helplessness can lead to a fruitless ideological power struggle with often no side emerging the winner.

Worldviews can also clash in the diagnostic field, as in the case of a woman who had been complaining for weeks of a severe pain below her left costal arch, as well as loss of appetite. Laboratory tests, together with a sonography, gastroscopy, colonoscopy, and a CT scan were all inconclusive, causing the family doctor to rule out further examinations and to tell her that she was "not ill, but in perfect health". Although she was still suffering from pain, the patient was distraught, embarrassed, and felt that she had almost been stamped as a liar. She decided to get a second opinion and was greatly relieved to find that this time, the doctor took her seriously, even though she was told that unfortunately, she could not locate the cause of her pain with the methods currently available to her. This made the patient feel heard, for instead of claiming that her pain did not exist, it had become clear that the source could not be identified. Some physicians find it difficult to adopt such an attitude and take to judging what they are unfamiliar with, do not recognize or have never applied. Desperate and chronically ill people who ask their practitioners what they think of shamans, homeopathy, or energy healing are commonly met with "Oh, that's all humbug!" Such responses often cause patients to clam up on the topic in future, depriving physicians of the opportunity to openly discuss risks and benefits. Should, on the other hand, doctors candidly admit a lack of knowledge about a certain topic about which they are skeptical, and encourage patients to discuss their hopes and expectations, or address possible risks together, an element of trust is created which allows the patient to talk about something that the doctor might not approve of. Patients can be supported in this way while trying out new approaches and talking about their experiences in an open manner. What is more, feelings of hope, faith, and expectation are respected and not devalued or destroyed at the outset – something that is immensely important in the healing process.

Statistical evidence is also a challenge for doctors, therapists, and patients alike, raising the question as to whether this makes people feel more protected or threatened. A high statistical probability of surviving a disease will reassure a sick person, whereas a probability in the region of zero will be perceived as threatening and constitutes a stressor that might render recovery more difficult. However, statistics are statements and calculations involving greater numbers, they do not reveal anything about subjective fate. We never know exactly which part of a statistical survey reflects the individual, as in the case of a cancer patient faced with a statistically highly unfavorable survival prognosis which placed her under great emotional stress. One day, Grimm's fairy tale "Godfather Death" came to her mind out of the blue and she decided to reread it. She found herself becoming very agitated, as the fairy tale suggests that death can be outwitted and one's lifespan extended. From then on, the woman vowed not to believe medical advice, but in the possibilities outlined in the story, and ended up living not only the few months predicted by statistical calculations, but in fact several decades.

3.

Understanding Illness in Analytical Psychology

3.1 The Shadow Concept and its Significance for Psychosomatics

What happens when people fall ill? A woman, confronted with a cancer diagnosis, describes her immediate reaction as follows: "I felt as if I had been struck a heavy blow. As if something hugely unfamiliar had entered my life without my noticing" (*translated from the German original*) (van Heyst 1982, 22).

Basically, fascination with the unknown can lure people into adventure, but it can also be frightening or provoke aggression. Cancer is something material and hylic, which grows and proliferates in us. It certainly belongs to us, having developed from our healthy cells, but we nevertheless experience "malignant" tumor cells as foreign, and we do not want them inside us. We frequently react with disbelief when we learn that we have a serious disease. We express how foreign an illness is to us by exclaiming: "How could this have happened, I've never had this before!"

The idea of something foreign entering the human body is an old one. Since the early days of humanity, illness was thought of as an intrusion. Worms or foreign bodies, but especially spirits, would invade humans, where they spread and caused harm (Schipperges 1999, 7). While nowadays we still think of worms, viruses and bacteria as intruders, we tend to explore mental factors today to explain away spirits. However, in the context of mental illness, patients occasionally remark that they no longer know themselves, or have become strangers to themselves and others. Treatment methods are therefore required to help overcome or integrate this feeling of strangeness, and allow patients to return to the "realm of health" which they have fallen out of. Some people experience serious illness as a literal banishment to the "world of the sick" where unpleasant conditions prevail and have to be faced. A body attacked by disease can force a person to slow down, and demand attention and time in an era where time has become a precious commodity and we can little afford to slacken our pace. However, these concepts do not appear to be so new, and have long since found their way into everyday language: The German word *geschwind*, meaning *soon* and *fast*, shares the same linguistic root as the German *gesund* (= *healthy*). So even language seems to be aware of the fact that health is a prerequisite for people's ability to keep up with the tempo of modern life.

In Analytical Psychology anything foreign, bad, or evil is considered a shadow aspect. Negative personality traits and hidden, adverse characteristics belong to the shadow, as does everything else that is hidden from the ego: "*We do not see into it, we are an enigma to ourselves*" (Jung 1976, 18/1, §38). This shadow aspect can be irritating, perhaps because we find this side of ourselves hard to accept, and therefore block it out or suppress it.

Jung's shadow concept, however, does not only include psychic phenomena, but also extends to the body, which, after all, creates the shadow:

> We do not like to look at the shadow side of ourselves; therefore there are many people in our civilized society who have lost their shadow altogether, they have got rid of it. They are only two-dimensional; they have lost the third dimension, and with it they have usually lost the body. The body is a most doubtful friend because it produces things we do not like; there are too many things about the body which cannot be mentioned. The body is very often the personification of this shadow of the ego. Sometimes it forms the skeleton in the cupboard, and everybody naturally wants to get rid of such a thing. (Jung, CW 18/1, § 40)

To illustrate this with an example: many people avoid talking about bodily phenomena with the prefix "ex-", such as excrement, exudation, or expectoration. This desire to be rid of something unpleasant mentioned by Jung is ultimately reminiscent of anorexia, because anorexic patients wish for nothing more than to eliminate their bodies, which are unwanted and which they have declared war on. Anorexia is probably one of the most radical responses to the rejection of the body and its urges:

> Yet this body is a beast with a beast's soul, an organism that gives unquestioning obedience to instinct. To unite oneself with this shadow is to say yes to instinct, to this formidable dynamism lurking in the background. (Jung 1966, CW 7, §35)

The ego cannot escape physical drives, such as hunger or sexuality, which render us slaves to our bodies to a certain extent. This form of unfreedom has preoccupied humanity for a long time. We might find body approval difficult because this bondage is predominantly based on a long-standing tradition of rejection. The Greek philosopher Plato, for example, described his body as a prison, as something which deprives the mind of freedom (Schipperges 1999, 42). Similarly, the Indian sage Sri Ramana Maharshi (1879-1950) viewed his body as a troublesome lump which he is said to have severely neglected in his quest for enlightenment. His unwashed hair became a matted mass, and his fingernails were long and crooked, making his hands useless. He supposedly sat on one and the same spot for weeks, surrounded and bitten by swarming ants, which raised great concern among his followers (Zimmer 1954, 59). Later, the idea of liberating the unloved body was also taken up by Christianity's ascetic morality, which Jung saw as a "*risk of disorganizing man's animal nature at the deepest level*" (Jung 1966, CW 7, §35).

However, such strict asceticism as a means to achieving control of the entire body may also give rise to contradiction. Probably Jung's inability to come to terms with such loveless neglect of the body speaks to the heart of many people because "*beauty is one of the most excellent of God's creations*" (Jung 1958, CW 11, § 954).

In any case, Jung emphatically warned against believing spiritual and mental development as the ultimate goal, and felt that devaluating or even overcoming the body – as once demanded by Plato – was not to be desired. The vital importance of the body for self-development and self-realization in the context of the individuation process is evident for Jung:

> We conclude that meditative philosophy consists in the overcoming of the body by mental union [*unio mentalis*]. [...] This mental union was not the culminating

> point but merely the first stage of the procedure. The second stage is reached when the mental union, that is, the unity of spirit and soul, is conjoined with the body. (Jung 1963, CW 14/2, § 663f.)

In reflecting on our bodies, we touch not only upon our personal shadow, which largely coincides with the Freudian notion of the unconscious as the place where personal aspects are blocked out or suppressed – but also upon a transpersonal shadow. The idea of a transpersonal, collective shadow, and thus of everything that is collectively frowned upon and rejected, is closely linked to images of God and the devil. In the Biblical book of Job, for example, we encounter the power of this shadow in the form of the devil, who is regarded as one of the sons of God. Good and evil therefore both belong to the divine, an idea which was overridden in Christianity by the church fathers Origen and Augustine in the 4th century AD, and replaced with the new idea of a God as a "summum bonum," an exclusively good being, expressed as follows:

> Nothing evil was created by God; we ourselves have produced all wickedness." [...] And thus evil does not inhere in its own substance, but arises from the mutilation of the soul. [It is] a condition of the soul, [...] proceeding from light-minded persons. Each of us should acknowledge that he is the first author of the wickedness in him: wrong decision of will, delusion, evil desires and more. (Jung, CW 9/2, § 82ff)

Evil as a problem of human attitude for which humanity alone bears responsibility corresponds to the philosophical concept of the so-called "privatio boni." Jung rightly alludes to the fatality of this idea by arguing that if evil is the consequence of psychological negligence, it can virtually dissolve into nothingness – an attitude that he feels is generally too optimistic. Jung also doubted this idea because on a psychological level, good and evil are equivalent opposites that do not exist without consciousness. People do not classify only human impulses, but also natural phenomena into good and evil. Nature, however, is a fundamentally amoral self-regulating system that, without judgement, uses birth, disease, eating and being eaten to maintain its balance. To give an example: By sucking dry a host plant, an aphid displays a healthy behavior, because from the creature's point of view, weakening the plant is the right thing to do. The plant owner naturally sees this differently. Yet, "privatio boni" is about people's ethical attitude, underlying the idea that individuals are able to do what is good and right – if they only want to.

This concept has probably also influenced psychiatric models of illness. About 80 years before Freud's appearance, Professor Johann Heinroth (1773-1843) was awarded the first ever German chair of psychiatry at the University of Leipzig. He viewed mental disorders as a "voluntary surrender to evil," and in his main works[3] argues that they are the result of personal guilt: "*From it spring all evils, including the disorders of the life of the soul*" (*translated from the German original*) (quoted from Kraft 1986, 12f).

On an unconscious level, this idea is still effective today, even if no longer religiously justified. Those who see the psychic realm – as suggested by the idea of "privatio boni" and taken up by Heinroth – as controllable, for instance by means of discipline and good will, may experience feelings of shame, guilt, or failure when they do not succeed. This might also be a reason for the negative image that mental or psychosomatic illnesses still have today. Jung, however, claims that anyone

3. Manual of Mental Disorders („Lehrbuch der Störungen des Seelenlebens"), and Manual of Mental Healing („Lehrbuch der Seelenheilkunde").

who in accordance with "privatio boni" ascribes all power over the so-called evil or the unconscious of the soul to individuals, would be naïve and run the risk of overestimating the power of the ego, which is tantamount to hubris, i.e., negative inflation.

The latter is also found in some current psychosomatic concepts of illness, which indicate that the personal shadow, i.e., individual inadequacies, deficient personality maturation, or insufficient conflict resolution are the roots of illness. Thorwald Dethlefsen and Rüdiger Dahlke, authors much respected by lay people, write about cancer in this way in their book on alternative medicine which is recognized as a standard reference work:

> People have cancer because they are cancer. [...] The fallacy lies in the distinction between *I* and *You*. This creates the illusion that one can survive particularly well as an "I" by sacrificing the "You" and using it as a breeding ground. [...] Cancer shows unlived love, cancer is perverted love. [...] Whoever does not live this love in consciousness runs the risk of letting his love sink into physicality where it seeks to realize its laws in the form of cancer (*translated from the German original*). (Dethlefsen & Dahlke 2019, 342f)

Dethlefsen describes the cancer patient as an egoist who refuses to love, and consequently gets cancer, which can only be understood as a form of punishment. A corresponding link between character structure and cancer disease was also made by an oncologist as he approached the bedside of a patient suffering from breast cancer to inform her about chemotherapy: "Aggressive woman, aggressive cancer, aggressive therapy!"

These statements make us wonder if a person who has the ability to love deeply and dearly would therefore be spared from cancer; in the same way, would well-balanced people be spared from aggressive forms of the disease? This may indeed be doubted, because whoever believes in such theories not only carries the burden of the disease, but allegedly also personal guilt. I do not share this view, but agree with Verena Kast, who writes:

> We do not become ill because we have done something wrong, instead we might become ill when life enters a new situation. [...] It is not because we have done or failed to do something, that things happen the way they do; we live within circumstances where changes occur with which we can deal either well or badly. (Kast 1992, 131)

Yet, such an open and neutral attitude is still very difficult for most people to adopt nowadays, probably because they long for, or even need, an underlying cause to keep their world-view intact. Accepting the fact that disease may strike at any time would be tantamount to accepting nature as something unpredictable and amoral. Health would no longer be either an achievement or a merit, but rather a gift. Such experiences can often be disturbing, give rise to indignation, or even result in shock, if one's pursuit of a healthy lifestyle apparently does not bring about the expected benefits. It is probably for this reason that the aforementioned interpretations of illness are still popular today.

The perennial question of whether guilt is related to illness is also posed in the New Testament, when Jesus encounters a man blind from birth. When asked by his disciples whether the man's sins or that of his parents were the cause of his condition, Jesus replies that no one has sinned, that is, no one has done anything wrong, and illness must be understood as the work of God (John 9:1-3). This concept of illness was already reflected in Greek mythology, where we read that the god Apollo can trigger illness with the shot of an arrow, but likewise has healing powers. Psychologically speaking, illness and healing would be ascribed to divine forces, that is, fate, which is unavailable to humankind. Due to the progress we have made and our advanced knowledge of diseases, this is now no longer entirely the case and a field of tension has opened up between the potential influence of the ego and factors that must be accepted. This human sphere of influence was also acknowledged by Jesus, namely when he admonished a paralytic after healing him to sin no more, lest something worse befall him (John 5:14). It is therefore important to distinguish between the personal shadow and impersonal, collective shadow phenomena, which touch upon the Jungian concept of the Self.

3.2 The Concept of the Self and its Relevance for Psychosomatics

Ego-consciousness is not yet developed at birth. Every individual is a single entity, and it is only with the formation of ego consciousness that the psyche disintegrates so that an ego and complexes can emerge from the unconscious. In the course of life, during the individuation process, a person can merge and once again form a unity, which will, however, differ in that the conscious ego carefully observes the unconscious and remains related to it (von Franz 1999, 138).

Jung refers to this original unity and wholeness as the *Self*, which encompasses all conscious and unconscious phenomena by uniting inner opposites and personality traits. The Self is an inconceivable postulate because the unconscious can only be described in part and will, at least to some extent, always remain unrecognizable. It is experienced as the center of our being – an inner core, an inextinguishable spark or spiritus rector. It is personal and at the same time, reaches beyond our ego, with its symbols unfolding with a fascinating, yet shattering effect, making them practically indistinguishable from the image of God or the divine within us (Daniel, 2020).

What then is the connection between the image of God or the Divine and the body? Convinced of the animacy of the body, the alchemist Zosimos of Panopolis declared that God had fallen or descended into dark matter and that humanity must liberate or redeem the Divine (Jung 1958, CW 11, § 350). The church father Basilides likewise assumed that a third of the Revealed God was accommodated in the body, which would indeed attribute it with a considerable degree of holiness (Jung 1959, CW 9/2, § 120). In much the same light, St. Paul recommended praising the flesh, as he deemed the body to be a temple of God – a precious and divine gift that was meant to be loved. Orthodox Christianity also approved of matter because it enabled participation in the Divine after Christ had accepted and elevated matter by his incarnation.

The lowest part of the spine is the sacrum, also called os sacrum, meaning "sacred bone", which in the German language (*Kreuzbein*) is associated with an important religious symbol, namely the cross.[4] If this place were to be connected with divine mystery, then holiness would not be found in the lofty heights, for example in the brain with all its reasoning and understanding, but close to the darkest, most autonomous physical processes, linked to excretion and sexuality. Against this background, modern body cults could, at least partly, be seen in a different light: Are people in pursuit of body cults in search of this hidden divine without suspecting

4. *Translator's note*: German *Kreuz* = English *cross*

it, i.e., looking for it on an unconscious level? The word "cult" would be an indication that this could indeed be the case. The present-day desire for physical immortality should also be mentioned in this context. Alchemists were convinced that something elusive and precious and the secret of immortality lay hidden in the body. Their traditions reach as far back as ancient Egypt, when even then, adepts were trying to resurrect their bodies in their own lifetimes – which according to their conviction, could only be achieved by the grace of God. Similarly, the aim of Eastern meditation methods is to produce a "diamond body" during one's lifetime, to crystallize something indestructible – an idea whose real counterpart is found in nature: as soon as a foreign body enters a mussel, the latter reacts by secreting nacre to integrate the foreign substance and form a pearl, which will eventually survive the mussel. It therefore symbolizes the eternal, formed by a mortal living being. Those who see the pearl as a symbol of eternity should not forget that it was only created as a result of foreign intrusion. In psychological terms, working with the shadow would therefore symbolize the birth of immortal preciousness.

Jung was also convinced that the body is both the origin and home of the symbols of the collective unconscious, particularly those of the Self, characterized by their numinosity, rooting mysteriously in the darkness of matter, from where they are able to manifest themselves in physical and spiritual form:

> The symbols of the self arise in the depths of the body, and they express its materiality every bit as much as the structure of the perceiving consciousness. [...] The deeper "layers" of the psyche lose their individual uniqueness as they retreat farther and farther into

> darkness. "Lower down," that is to say as they approach the autonomous functional systems, they become increasingly collective until they are universalized and extinguished in the body's materiality [...] The more archaic and "deeper," that is the more *physiological*, the symbol is, the more collective and universal, the more "material" it is. (Jung 1959, CW 9/1, § 291)

What are the implications of these ideas for seriously ill people, their therapists, or relatives? Conscious and unconscious phantasies, emerging symbols and images can be indicative of the path to be followed, sometimes guiding decisions, or even alluding to prognoses. Archetypal images that have been valid for eons are a vessel in which human suffering, healing, and meaning, but also consolation and farewell can unfold – provided we are mindful and dare to connect with them.

After suffering a heart attack, Jung had impressive dreams and, among other things, saw himself in a pomegranate orchard, celebrating his wedding. He referred to this dream by saying: "*I was the marriage*" (quoted from Jaffé 1973, 294). This marriage motif is not only replicated in the dreams of the dying, but also in the ancient custom of dressing the deceased in their wedding suits. This ties in with the provocative request of Swiss psychiatrist Alfred Ziegler (Ziegler 2000, 35) that one should marry the abominable features of every terrible illness in a kind of "death wedding." By this, he suggests showing an unconditional engagement with the monstrosity of illness, instead of fighting it as a foreign body. Ziegler opines that this could lead to a feeling of vastness and eternity, although the idea may sound bizarre. A person's life becomes unique only because of its particular limitations, which can strangely enough give rise to an intense feeling of freedom. This is exactly what therapist Sue Austin described during a therapeutic process with a patient:

> However, our years of careful listening to her self-hatred and shame and sitting with the grief embedded in them, eventually gave way to an increasing capacity to tolerate and accept her powerlessness. Paradoxically, in that there was a degree of freedom. (Austin 2016b, 427)

Daring to relate to the terrible or incomprehensible in this way may generate a feeling of comfort and security where we would least expect it. Security is then occasionally experienced where uncertainty ought to be prevalent, either because we lack control, are afraid, or feel overwhelmed.

By engaging with difficulty in this way, we are also letting go. According to Ziegler, being in touch with one's individual idiosyncrasies can not only create an inviolable sense of security, but oddly enough, likewise alter physical illness. That which has materialized can be retransformed into the spiritual, resublimed as it were. This again draws on the abovementioned alchemical image of "solve et coagula", in which meditation and imagination intervene in the cycle of material changes (Jung 1968, CW 12, § 394) – an idea which coincides with the findings of the association studies presented above, of placebo research as well as the effects of autogenic training or biofeedback.

Somewhat more fact-based than Alfred Ziegler, but in similar fashion, homeopath and Jungian analyst Edward Whitmont calls upon us to enter into a conscious partnership with our complexes and biological deficiencies. These should neither be denied nor suppressed, nor allowed to overwhelm us, which to his mind can be a truly terrifying task (Whitmont 1993, 139).

3.3 Meaningful Disease

Science-based medicine explores diseases predominantly by means of randomized trials and provides statistics on causal factors of disease. In archetypal medicine, on the other hand, the focus of interest is on the subject and the symbolic meaning of symptoms – individual idiosyncrasies and uniqueness are what matter. Hence, the two approaches and views are complementary. So far, archetypal medicine has grappled with the fact that it cannot provide objective evidence in the same way as science-based medicine does. It is based on inner evidence, on what is plausible, on subjective certainty and the experience of meaningfulness, all of which have an impact on the ongoing struggle to be taken seriously. In my opinion, anyone who is serious about holistic medicine needs to take on both of these complementary perspectives, a view shared by psychoneuroimmunologist Christian Schubert. By using very elaborate single case studies, he researches the connection between subjective experience and the immune system in everyday life, outside of laboratory conditions, as these cannot mirror the complexity of real-life situations. In these "Life as it is lived" studies, the entirety of the subjects' external experiences and related personal feelings, thoughts, and judgments, as well as their interaction with the immune system are recorded with great detail and precision (Schubert/Amberger 2019, 24) (see Chapter 4.2 Victim and Perpetrator as Complex Poles and their Significance for Psychosomatics).

According to Ziegler (Ziegler 2000), archetypal medicine uses analogies, as well as personal and mythical images emerging from intuition. It looks at tensions of opposites within us to trace the essence of mental and physical diseases. He holds that dark, alien personality features, maladjustments, inferiorities, or repression – and thus, the personal and/or collective shadow – appear to have a particular inclination to manifest in the body. An unconscious mental state thus plunges into matter and metamorphoses into a physical disease (Ziegler 2000, 22), as the shadow aspect comes to light in the form of a materially visible phenomenon.

On a therapeutic level, archetypal medicine relies, above all, on the effective power of language, because it is "*a psychosomaticum par excellence*" (Ziegler 2000, 41). Talk is akin to touch, as we see, e.g., when patients or therapists suddenly get goose bumps, wince, or feel exhausted, yet physically lighter or free from pain, among other things.

However, language can only have a psychosomatic effect if it touches the archetypal (image) level, that is, the level in the collective unconscious where matter and idea become identical (Ziegler 2000, 42). This happens when meaning is found, which might come as a shock to people or hit them on a deeply emotional level. In which way this affects us physically, however, remains a mystery.

Archetypal images are not as subjective as postulated above – as this claim would be paradoxical – but defined as typical human phenomena normally found in a certain context throughout the ages. They are collectively valid life patterns or life developments which are simply a given and cannot be explained. The trick is to find the pattern which is currently valid for the individual (or Zeitgeist), and this should not be done in a hasty or too general manner.

The archetypal image of rheumatoid arthritis deals with mobility and its opposite, which is stiffness or irreversibility. The archetypal conflict may then indicate a discrepancy between the two poles of sacrifice on the one hand, and respect for one's own needs on the other. Arthritis may prompt affected persons to ask themselves how they are dealing with issues of altruism versus egoism.

These images become evident in a case study carried out by psychoneuroimmunologist Brian Broom, who reported a 45-year-old female patient who was suffering from rheumatoid arthritis and exhibited the typical swelling and crippling of numerous joints. The usual drug treatments, including gold therapy, had not brought about any improvement. The disease had emerged at a time when the patient was feeling very "stuck" and "tied down" in her marriage, and her rheumatism echoed this by also "slowing her down". Eight months after separating – a step that had proved to be very difficult for her – her symptoms had subsided to such an extent that psychotherapy could be terminated. Six years later, she was doing amazingly well, both physically and emotionally, which she attributed to finding her true self in therapy (Broom 2015, 365f). Because the feeling of being stuck and immobile in her private life had also manifested itself in the patient's body, Broom speaks about a somatic metaphor. In this concept, the soul manifests itself in the body and the symptom serves as a meaningful symbol.

Broom also presents the case of a 60-year-old man who had been suffering from severe dermatitis of the face since the age of 20. The disease had emerged shortly after a family dispute in which he felt he had been cheated out of his inheritance, the family's farm. He took revenge by buying the property immediately adjacent, which left him "*permanently staring in the face*" of injustice (*exact wording, translated from the German original,* Broom 2015, 367), meaning that his anger and bitterness had not only become a constant mental affliction, but also a physical one. Writing about this more than 40 years ago, Ziegler demonstrated that anger or love can become visible in a reddening of the skin (Ziegler 2000, 20), which this case is consistent with. Broom's patient seemed relieved to have found a meaningful explanation for his condition, as well as concrete instructions for treatment – interestingly enough, his skin rash improved as soon as he took an extended trip for a long period, putting the family farm out of his sight.

It was only by incorporating subjective feelings, life experiences and conflicts, and the meaningful images gained from these, that treatment turned out to be successful in both these cases of severe inflammatory disease. Since Broom understands a physical disease as a somatic representation of the patient's life experience, and not as a mechanical connection between the psyche and the brain, he rejects the idea of talking about defense mechanisms in this context.

However, the concept of meaningful images – referred to by Broom as somatic metaphors – is refuted by many physicians, therapists, and even psychoneuroimmunologists because there appears to be no plausible explanation. Broom points out that all those who choose to adopt either a dualistic view or a materialistic monistic position will not in fact find a satisfactory answer, as symbols originate in the mind. He further holds that individual life consists of a mysterious dual aspect of physicality and subjectivity from the outset, which to my mind corresponds to the Jungian concept of synchronicity, i.e., the material and the psychical manifesting themselves simultaneously with meaning becoming visible in the body during this process.

We also learn about a 30-year-old female patient who was able to detect meaning behind a recent hearing loss, triggered by an infectious disease which made everyday communication more and more difficult for her. The woman felt increasingly isolated from her colleagues, friends, and family, but came to the painful realization that this isolation was not new at all. Having grown up as an only child, she had rejected certain parental values and attitudes to life at a very young age, and had therefore experienced herself as an excluded third party and had the impression that she and her parents were living in different worlds. The hearing loss triggered a similar situation, in which she felt anew what it meant to be excluded. This made her wonder, and she began to suspect that this had to do not only with a problem with her parents, but with a significant life issue, which she decided to address.

3.4 Anorexia – A Meaningful Disease

An important detail is to be found in the long tradition of bodily contempt, namely a collection of gnostic texts from the 2nd century, the Clementine Homilies, describing the good as the right male hand and the evil as the left female hand of God. The texts also state that "*the body comes from the female, who is characterized by emotionality; the spirit comes from the male, who stands for rationality*" (cited after Jung 1959, CW 9/2 §100). Here, we find a direct expression of the linkage between the female – physical – emotional – evil, which holds true for every human body, regardless of gender. The rejection of the body and its natural needs, as well as the feminine, is observed in many religions.

In today's Western world, many people, even believers, dismiss such a view. Yet asceticism is still very much in vogue, supposedly no longer for religious, but for worldly reasons, be it beauty or health. At great expense, with the aid of fasting, sport, or medical support, we attempt to bring our physical bodies more in line with the current ideal of slimness. But asceticism and discipline cannot be completely secular, because morally speaking, they continue to be strongly charged as virtues and expressions of spiritual strength and willpower. The ego of the anorexic person seems fascinated by this ascetic ideal.

A higher number of girls or women is affected by anorexia in comparison to men, which makes it all the more worth our while to look at the specifics of the female body, since women and men experience their bodies in significantly different ways. Whereas female ovulation signifies the willingness to incorporate something foreign in order to make new life possible, menstruation unquestionably denotes failure to conceive. Women who ardently desire a baby react to the onset of menstruation with disappointment, perhaps even despair, whereas those who wish to remain independent feel relieved. Indeed, to this day, pregnancy and the birth of a child signify a certain loss of autonomy for women, who must sacrifice a slice of their independence and personal freedom. In today's Western world, a woman who is not pregnant can live her life as freely as a man for whom this privilege used to be reserved. And it is still difficult nowadays for women to reconcile family, career, and personal interests. Depending on their attitude to life, women will therefore also view menopause differently. A woman who feels happy knowing she will never become pregnant again can enjoy increased freedom as her children grow up, and ages in a different way to a woman who experiences the increasing independence of her children or the impossibility of further pregnancy as a painful loss.

Even though with the aid of contraception, abortion, or social freezing, women are no longer fully at the mercy of biological processes, menstruation breaks into their lives at puberty with all its psychological and physical consequences. Therefore, one could say that an anorexic girl strives unconsciously towards the death of her body in order to prevent the symbolic death of her girlhood. In fact, with her asceticism, she creates an "opus contra naturam", for menstruation and the womanhood that goes with it are prevented. She can remain a girl. In a clinic, this physical regression of anorexia patients is integrated into treatment in a very concrete way. Initially, therapy is targeted at the bodily symptoms of severely underweight 10-13 year old girls, who are treated like infants, in keeping with their low weight. They have to lie down in bed and are fed in a loving, but firm way. Food is non-negotiable. If they spit out food or press their lips together to avoid eating, like healthy toddlers, it takes oodles of patience and loving persistence to break through their refusal. Plastic utensils normally reserved for toddlers are used and patients are washed, lotioned, and have their hair styled. Physical affection is given high priority, and the girls learn to allow their mothers to hug them. After 6-12 months, many of the girls are doing visibly better – and show less resistance to a number of pleasant physical sensations. After a year of treatment, one girl demonstrated the rediscovered enjoyment of her body with her happy dancing. As the basic etymological meaning of playing is actually dancing, we again encounter the healing power of the art of playfulness in this context, through which a new love of life can be found.

If Franz Kafka's short story "A Hunger Artist", first published in German in 1922 (Kafka 2015), were to be interpreted in terms of anorexia, we would discover that the art of starvation is truly not an easy one and attracts great public interest. The starving artist is a major attraction; everyone pays to marvel at him and touch his lean limbs. Guards testify that he starves himself as no one has ever done before and never eats anything secretly. This story confirms that starvation is admired in some societies as a highly recognized achievement. Anorexics also demonstrate that they welcome asceticism and can practice it to a greater extent than anyone else, but the external recognition or appreciation they crave is denied to them once they have become too thin. In Kafka's narrative, the hunger artist's guards can be seen as representing inner-soul personality traits (the animus in Jungian terminology) that support the ego in adhering to discipline. However, the guards also symbolize the bondage of the starving ego, which is why Kafka's hunger artist consequently sits in a cage, an image that Hilde Bruch took up in 1978 in her well-known book "The Golden Cage – The Enigma of Anorexia Nervosa." The fanaticism of starvation described by Kafka also depicts an unfree ego and, from the point of view of Analytical Psychology, the archetypal nature of asceticism. The ego is under the spell of a collective idea from which it can no longer distance itself, it has no choice, it must starve.

As mentioned above, Jung emphasized the connection between illness and Zeitgeist (Jung 1966, CW 7, § 18). The individual falls ill with the collective shadow problem and tries to solve it, but although the illness affects the individual, it is also part of society and its conflicts. In this sense, Doris Lier (Lier 2001, 8) understands anorexia as only one aspect of the mental condition of the 20th century, which she describes as an anorexic epoch, because of society's fascination with the plethora of streamlining processes. This is manifest in architecture, for example, with its minimalist skeletal building structures, in light, airy design, or in so-called "lean production" in the economy. However, the collective fascination with streamlining processes is not a decision of free will, but rather triggered by a process in the collective unconscious which puts the ego at its service. In this respect, we are not free in our fascination, which usually does not bother us as long as we feel good about it.

Therefore, it is not surprising that Kafka's hunger artist suffers just as little from his hunger prison as anorexics do. He is even dissatisfied with himself because he constantly wonders how he could starve himself even more. His gloomy state of mind can be compared to that of the depressed anorexic. He has an inner urge to constantly improve, and thus enhance his fasting performance, which reminds us of modern society's popular default obsession with self-optimization. Satisfaction is frowned upon because it is confused with stagnation. Optimization has become a social imperative according to the motto: "Perfect is the enemy of good". It permeates almost all areas of our lives and can be witnessed in the life-threatening, and thus shadowy, aspect of the downward spiral in anorexia through the stages "slim model" – "thin model" – "thinnest model" – "thin model dead" (Gramich 2019, 58).

Things become tragic for Kafka's hunger artist when society no longer shows interest in him because new, far more exciting attractions abound. One could say that fashion has changed because other phenomena seem more fascinating. Starvation is out, which is why the starving artist is no longer noticed and eventually even becomes forgotten. This also holds true for anorexia, about which not much has been heard over the past two decades, although it is still a very common and life-threatening psychosomatic illness.

Before his death, Kafka's hunger artist was still able to reason that he was starving himself because he could not find anything he liked to eat. Tragically, it is only shortly before his death that he suspects there might not only be physical, but also spiritual nourishment. Perhaps he should have rejected certain collective spiritual-soul values instead of material food. But it is too late for Kafka's hunger artist to figure this out, as it is for about 30% of anorexics who die from their illness. According to Lier, anorexia is also difficult to cure because we live in an era whose mental makeup is in fact anorexic and shares the values of anorexics in many ways (Lier 2001, 44). In her view, there is a danger that psychiatry, just like sufferers, will become entrenched in a battle of the opposing parties of body and mind. Whereas anorexia sufferers do their utmost to eradicate the ephemeral, psychiatry tries to make them regain a sense of pleasure in their bodies and so rather devalues the spiritual or intellectual. As a result, those involved remain stuck in a usually fruitless struggle or power mode. The spontaneous healings which have been documented show that the key to recovery often lies in the ability to love and be loved, and to be devoted, which can help the illness fade into the background.

Before healing becomes possible, an uphill struggle may well be necessary, as the fairy tale "The Enchanted Princess" (Zaunert 1964, 144) demonstrates. The protagonist is only willing to marry a suitor who can solve her riddles. After many men have already died because they failed at this task, a young man called Peter comes forward and wants to make the next attempt. He is aided by the ghost of a deceased man whose funeral expenses he paid. The ghost knows that the princess is under the spell of a mountain spirit whom she visits at night and who wants to possess her all to himself. Peter has to accompany the princess on her nightly excursions three times, each time beating her with a rod. The fairy tale stipulates that his heart bleeds while he is beating her, making it obvious that he is averse to doing so, and not sadistically inclined. He obeys on behalf of his ghost. The mountain spirit, on the other hand, takes pleasure in tormenting people according to the fairytale, and wants the princess to kill this suitor as well. Only in this way can she become what he regards as pure so that he can own her. If we relate this narrative to anorexia, it becomes apparent that a male spirit wants to keep young women away from any relationship with human males, men of flesh and blood. And so they remain pure, a characteristic of virginity, which is very highly valued in many cultures.

Interestingly, the cave of the mountain spirit also contains an altar, a table on which religious sacrifices are offered, signifying that questions of faith and God are involved, as well as religious questions of collective importance, since the story is about a princess.

Bernd Gramich (Gramich 2019, 79) questions to what extent the Self might play a role in anorexia, especially in cases where therapy fails. According to this fairy tale, it would be a numinous male spirit demanding the princess to forego any relationship with human males. In the struggle with her own body, this sacrifice seems possible, and as a bodiless, angelic being, the woman could ultimately belong entirely to the realm of the mountain spirit. But this would only be possible with physical death and the abandonment of this world.

In the fairy tale, young Peter hides behind the altar of the mountain spirit and learns the respective answers to the riddles. On his first visit, the mountain spirit asks the princess to think of her father's white horse, on the second visit, to think of his sword, and the third time, the mountain spirit chooses his own head. Thus, the riddles are always related to thinking, and moreover, solely to the world of the king or the mountain spirit. The mother does not play a role in the matter, nor does any other woman. And in this case, salvation is provided by the male spirit, and not by the female, nurturing or sensual realm. Healing therefore comes about in accordance with the homeopathic principle of "Like cures like".

At the behest of his companion ghost, Peter must cut off the mountain spirit's head on his third visit and bring it to the king and the princess the next morning. The most important step on the way to the princess' redemption is now completed: she is freed and can marry Peter. According to the fairy tale, the mountain spirit cannot be negotiated with, but has to die because that which takes pleasure in killing humans and their ability to relate to others must itself be eliminated. So something inside a sick woman has to die and this is, according to the fairy tale, a painful journey. In therapy, therefore, it may take aggression, and imposition to a certain degree, to break the mental spell under which an anorexic woman or even an anorexic man find themselves. Being imposed upon causes both mental and physical pain, because it brings about contact with something that needs to be overcome. The body becomes perceptible, albeit in an unpleasant way. In a therapeutic context, this can mean not permitting patients to distract themselves by thinking only about food. It can be very helpful to actively interrupt these kinds of thoughts because, to stay in the language of the fairy tale, it is the only way to break the power of the mountain spirit. Gramich demonstrates that there may be circumstances under which it is admissible to place demands on female patients in the healing process, and how calming and relieving such "painful" interventions can be for them. In this regard, Cord Benecke speaks of the "empathic meanness" of the therapist (Benecke 2018, 28). He uses this term for interventions in which therapists "push" their patients into unwanted directions, asking them to confront their terrible, painful feelings instead of avoiding them, to name just a few points. Even if Benecke was not referring to psychosomatic processes in this context when he uttered that "*from a psychodynamic point of view, clinically sustainable changes cannot be expected without substantial changes in the individual emotional system*" (*translated from the German original*) (Benecke 2018, 28), it can be assumed that on the basis of what has been said so far, physical changes also take place in a therapeutic process like this.

However, some therapists find this kind of intervention difficult because they themselves perceive negative emotions as unsettling. Still, painful interventions can be advantageous and thus, beneficial, because patients observe therapists dealing with their own shadows in a positive way.

Digression: Women's and Men's Health

It was not so long ago that physicians swore the Hippocratic Oath which began with the following lines: "I swear to Apollo the physician and Asclepius and Hygieia and Panacea and call all the gods and goddesses to witness..."

Western medicine thus invokes Greek mythology, and to this day, the symbol of the medical profession is represented by the staff of Asclepius entwined with a serpent. It depicts the Greek god of healing Asclepius, son of the Greek god Apollo, and a mortal woman. Even if doctors are occasionally referred to as demigods in white in modern times, their role model is to be found in Asclepius, who was half man and half god, and who made medical knowledge accessible to humankind. Previously, it had been the gods, first and foremost Apollo, who could cause and cure illness. Diseases were thus of divine origin and healing also lay in the hands of the divine according to the homeopathic principle: "*He who wounds also heals*" (Kerényi, 1998, 23), which can be traced back to Apollo.

The medicine offered by Asclepius was less active and mostly one of little intervention. Mentally or physically ill persons had to travel to his temple, cleanse themselves and wait in the temple for healing by sleeping. Thus, above all, devotion, waiting, and hope were required. Healing took place at night-time and in dreaming after retreating from one's fellow humans to a suitably sacred place. Healing had its origin inside a person, whose deepest layers had to be touched in order to make epiphany possible. Each sick person would go on their individual healing journey, thus allowing an inner healing spring to bubble up. In the language of Analytical Psychology, we speak about the direct experience of the self opening up to the ego and vice versa.

Professional specialization came about with the wife and the children of Asclepius. His sons Machaon (the butcher), Polemocrates (the master of war) and Nicomachus (the one who is victorious in battle) fought in the Trojan War. They wounded others, yet at the same time, worked as so-called barber surgeons, meaning that they united warlike character traits with the positive qualities of a physician in one person, well versed in both the practical and the scientific aspects of their profession (Kerényi 1998, 50). Such warlike drive is still required in medicine today, especially when it comes to life-threatening diseases, and is reflected in the terms "steel and beam" as synonyms for surgery and radiation.

The women in Asclepios' family were also medical practitioners, with knowledge and practice in the use of nature's healing substances. Asclepius' wife Epione (the soothing one) was responsible for pain relief, his daughter Hygieia (health) for hygiene and prevention, and his daughter Panacea (the all-healing one) for healing with plants, juices, and compresses. These feminine healers all exuded patience when treating chronic illnesses, which sometimes cannot be cured, but only alleviated. They knew what kind of lifestyle could help prevent disease, and were also aware of the healing power of music. The balanced reference to two male and two female healing beings in the Hippocratic Oath is striking. From our perspective today, the male and female medical specialties of these myths could be interpreted as the invasive (conventional) medicine versus the gentle (alternative) medicine. Nowadays, these two streams tend to devalue or even run counter to instead of complement each other, as required by the Hippocratic Oath.

3.5 Pain – A Meaningful Syndrome

In the above-mentioned fairy tale "The Enchanted Princess", inflicting pain was a necessary building block towards healing, which in turn led to liberation from a spirit hostile to life. Almost every illness limits personal freedom in some way, for example, a food allergy denies us the freedom to eat everything we want to eat; a body ache robs us of the freedom to do all that we want to do, perhaps even the ability to fall asleep or sleep through the night. Therefore, it goes without saying that anyone suffering from physical or emotional pain would like to be free of it.

But how does one get rid of it? The German word *Pein* for pain, like the English word *pain*, stems from the Latin *poena* or from the Greek *poine*, meaning penalty, ransom payment, debt redemption, as well as chastisement and punishment. If we take pain to mean "debt redemption", then this raises questions of morality and shadow, but also the theme of money in the German language. In this context, scientists in Pittsburgh carried out a study comparing the brain activity of test persons when using different methods of payment. Cash payments triggered greater activity in precisely the parts of the brain where our sense of pain is perceived. However, when payments were made by credit card, then the pain center remained completely calm. Researchers call this phenomenon "the pain of paying". When paying with cash, a physical act of separation or loss occurs which causes discomfort to varying degrees. When using a credit card, on the other hand, people do not experience a sense of loss and are happy to spend more. It can thus hurt to spend money, but using a credit card can prevent the pain of loss for many people. Researchers found that credit cards produce an effect similar to a numbing injection (Kremer 2013; Zellermayer 1996). This interconnection between money, pain and redemption was already apparent in ancient times, when pain was said to have had the same kind of character as a monetary transaction. Pain was viewed as a kind of currency which was passed back and forth between the gods and humans, with a certain amount of pain being offered to the gods in order to stave off far more unbearable suffering (Morris 1991, 71).

The neurobiologically proven connection between separation, loss, and pain applies not only to money, but also on a more general level: experiences of loss and deprivation are a dispositional factor in the development of chronic pain, from which, by the way, about 15% of the population currently suffers (Ermann 2016, 306). It is therefore important for chronic pain patients to search back in their minds to their first experience of major loss prior to the onset of their pain disorder, as this experience leaves its mark on all of us and usually reactivates our worst primal perception of abandonment and loss. Indeed, the greatest threat to all babies, both human and mammalian, is loss or separation from the mother, as she is indispensable to their survival, and nurtures and protects them while growing. Babies cry and animals yelp or squeak to summon the mother. When children or animals grow a bit bigger, they begin to actively seek out the mother.

Separation from the mother causes a drop in endogenous opioids, the painkillers produced by the body to relieve pain, without which separation and loss are truly painful. The mental pain of separation is a physical pain. The difference between physical – "real" – and mental pain is probably not as great as many people think, but mental pain cannot simply be labelled as "imagination".

According to Marie-Louise von Franz, loss is also a major factor in alcohol dependence (von Franz 1986, 30). In her experience, many alcohol abusers have experienced perceived or real abandonment and often feel unloved and alone. This may not always be true in reality, although a feeling of abandonment may still persist. This experience of abandonment, she believes, is one reason for the success of Alcoholics Anonymous, who provide the sympathetic attention and security needed to get over the pain of abandonment. Since abandonment and loss are accompanied by pain, and alcohol is a time-honored anesthetic or painkiller, alcohol consumption can be viewed as an unconscious attempt at self-healing – usually ending in self-destruction. In light of this interrelationship, the UK government's announcement in 2018 to appoint a Minister for Loneliness appears to be an important step forward in public health. From a depth psychology perspective, however, the issues at hand have to do not only with one's relationship with people, animals, and the outside world, but also with one's own soul, the Self, and the Divine.

Experiences of loss are stressors and play a role in the development of allergic reactions (Ermann 2016, 371), which akin to pain, force us to restrict and renunciate certain varieties of food, substances or materials which may be harmful. The fact that loss is not only painful, but plays an important role in the development of allergies illustrates that psychosomatic illness cannot be attributed to any one organ or symptom, but only to certain "trends" that can be described. However, certain parallels between allergies and pain do exist: pain is not only felt, but is a thwarting, frustrating, confusing, weakening, and above all, an isolating factor, which takes priority and prevents us from participating in the diverse entertainment options available, such as going to the movies, driving, or hiking. In this respect, both pain and allergies extort a sacrifice, demanding that we withdraw from the world and bid farewell to every excess in life.

Feelings of loss and abandonment can be expressed physically in three different ways, namely through pain, allergic reaction, or alcohol addiction. Yet, a clear reverse conclusion is not possible, because loss and abandonment are not necessarily the cause of the three syndromes.

Even if we identify the cause of our pain, our approach to dealing with it is shaped by Zeitgeist-dependent theological, cultural, economic, scientific, or psychological concepts (Morris 1991, 68). In his US study in 1969, for example, anthropologist Mark Zborowski determined that the attitude of male war veterans towards pain depended on which ethnic group they belonged to. Among the four groups interviewed, namely Irish, Jewish, Italian, and American (resident for at least three generations), he discovered that certain ethnicities conveyed their pain expressively and without inhibition, while others tended to hide their pain and withdraw. Based on his research, he concluded that people respond to pain not only as individuals, but also as members of an ethnic group. The way pain is experienced is at least partially influenced by the value that one's social group attributes to it. While for some ethnic groups, pain is a source of pride and a call to bear things heroically, other groups see pain as a punishment for sins committed and a test of one's faith, to name just two views.

This is reminiscent of the results of Jung's association studies (Jung 1972, CW 2, § 999), which he conducted together with his colleagues in the form of a word association test on a total of about 100 persons in 24 families. It was shown that persons related to each other show considerable similarities in complex patterns, with children being more likely to be closer to the mother than the father. Even though the study only considers a small number of cases, this historical experiment already proved at its time that complex landscapes are shaped by milieu, and that affective attitudes and complex patterns are handed down by parents.

These historical studies are no longer transferable today in terms of topical attitudes, yet the question arises as to what extent family and collective disease complexes continue to be effective. Current findings suggest that they still are, as documented by Michael Ermann who describes a frequently encountered neurotic family linkage in pain disorders (Ermann 2016, 305). As physical diseases nowadays continue to run in families, addressing family or cultural complexes and conflicts often promotes health and alleviates pain.

If no effective pain treatment is available, paying attention to circumstances that have a favorable effect on pain intensity and pain progression may be worthwhile – something Immanuel Kant took to heart. With no effective conventional medical therapy available in the 18th century for his extremely painful attacks of gout, he found relief in concentration. As soon as pain surfaced, he concentrated on a mental topic with all his might and worked on it. Kant thus actively introduced a theme into his field of consciousness, leaving little energy and attention for the perception of pain. This method was so successful that he is occasionally said not to have known in the morning whether he had suffered pain during the night or not (Morris 1991, 17). Doing what he was best at, i.e., thinking, which Kant also enjoyed, altered his pain. Even today, some pain patients observe that rest or taking things easy does not contribute significantly to the relief of pain, sometimes making it even worse. Contrary to popular belief, they find to their surprise that certain activities diminish the pain, making it recede into the background. One chronic pain patient, for example, was surprised to find her pain lessened significantly whenever she started singing songs from her homeland. Therefore, it is important to find out how many activities, and which ones, can influence pain favorably; this usually turns out to be what you like doing and what you are good at.

The American journalist Norman Cousins also embarked on a very personal search for pain relief (Strobel 1990, 39) after he fell ill with extremely painful ankylosing spondylitis in 1964. Not only was his spine affected, but he also suffered from paralysis, and doctors gave him a 1:500 chance of survival. This poor prognosis was understandably an emotional shock to him. After reading that a largely negative mood would also have a negative effect on his body, he began to wonder whether a positive mood could, conversely, have a positive influence on physical processes. In search of a mood enhancer, he came up with the idea of watching comedy movies and reading funny books. Just ten minutes of convulsive laughter dispelled his pain, and he was able to catch some restful sleep. As soon as the pain resumed, he watched the next movie. A few months later, he was able to get out of bed, return to work, and do some sports. His unusual recovery attracted a lot of attention and was the impetus for research on therapeutic humor. Because laughter had helped him, he later developed laughter therapy. Some 50 years after Cousin's own experience, psychoneuroimmunological studies demonstrated that cheerfulness, joy, and laughter were significant factors in lowering the inflammation levels of rheumatoid arthritis in patients (Schubert/Amberger 2019, 176).

Based on his recovery, Cousins also concluded that embedded in one's inner subjective truth, every person has a self-healing ability which is there to be developed, and once it has been discovered, one requires courage to cast aside conventional ideas and do what is best for oneself to remain personally consistent. People who, like Norman Cousins in 1964, stop all medication and leave hospital to devote themselves entirely to laughter are easily seen as irrational or even irresponsible. The ego needs the strength to withstand such reproaches and not allow itself to be deflected from its chosen path. Like Norman Cousins, others have developed therapy methods based on their own spectacular healing journeys and have subsequently helped numerous people. However, if we take seriously the ability to self-heal as an expression of one's own inner configuration, then it holds that imitating something that has worked for others will not necessarily work for us too. This would at least offer a partial explanation for the odysseys that numerous patients undergo from one form of therapy to the next and why they become more and more desperate because nothing really helps them. When external recommendations fail to match up to one's inner subjective truth, they cannot be effective. Once this point has been reached, courage is needed to search wholly within oneself, for example, in introspection, dreams, imagination, or open play and curiosity. Here, we are talking about exploring one's phantasies, no matter how crazy or absurd they may be. Anyone who dares to contradict common sense, quickly experiences resistance, which is why Jung's assessment remains thought-provoking to this day:

> To think otherwise than as our contemporaries think is somehow illegitimate and disturbing; it is even indecent,

> morbid or blasphemous, and therefore socially dangerous for the individual. [...] To allow the soul or psyche a substantiality of its own is repugnant to the spirit of the age, for that would be heresy. (Jung 1969, CW 8, § 653)

This kind of inner conflict was a deciding factor in the case of a 54-year-old woman who had been complaining for days about persistent severe pain in her lower left canine tooth. Routine examinations provided no clues as to the cause, which left her dentist of many years at a loss. As he did not want to start any hasty treatment, he asked his patient if anything had happened in the last few days. It transpired that the night before she first felt any pain, her sister had suffered acute paralysis due to an as yet undetected advanced cancer. As a result of this diagnosis, she was now requiring home health care and wanted her sister to nurse her until she died. The two sisters had always lived together alone in a large house, and the dentist's patient felt a moral duty to perform this labor of love for her sibling. Yet, at the same time, she felt a great internal resistance at having to give up her profession in order to provide this care. Her dentist advised her not to relinquish her standpoint in the matter too hastily, however difficult she might find this. He argued that it would not be in her sister's interest if she also started suffering because she was pining for her profession. Instead, a nurse could be hired. To her surprise, as well as that of her dentist, the patient's tooth complaint vanished completely after this short conversation and no dental treatment was required (Strobel 1990, 57). One could say that the patient was able to resolve her conflict in such a constructive manner that both her needs and that of her sibling were met to the best extent possible. Neither had to make too great a sacrifice. Conflict or ambivalence, then, can not only cause emotional, but also physical pain, which blocks or slackens the ego, invites it to listen inwardly and face inner reality. Pain can thus be the "start of finding oneself" (Böhme 2003, 95) and a source of awareness. This may sound cynical to people suffering from unbearable chronic pain, because they often experience the opposite, namely a kind of ego destruction which no longer makes a life-affirming attitude possible. Even if this is hard to swallow, we have to acknowledge that some pain is intractable, as Ricarda Huch states in her poem "*Nicht alle Schmerzen sind heilbar*" ("Not all pain is curable" – *translation from the German original)*

Not all pains are curable, for some creep
deeper and deeper into the heart,
And as days and years go by,
They become as stone.
You speak and laugh as if nothing were wrong,
They seem to melt away like foam.
But you feel their weight is heavy
Even in your dreams.
Spring comes again with warmth and brightness,
The world becomes a sea of blossoms.
But in my heart, there is a place
Where nothing blooms anymore.

4.

Therapeutic Aspects

4.1 The Complex and its Significance for Psychosomatics

In 1905, Jung performed the word association test on a 24-year-old female patient, who had grown up as the only daughter and youngest of five children, a total of six times during the initial outpatient consultation and subsequent inpatient treatment in order to objectify the course of therapy. In the second year of school, the patient developed generalized psychogenic jerks, during which she flailed, stomped, and occasionally emitted a scream. Her consciousness remained undisturbed during these seizures. Because of her symptomatology, she had to quit school at the age of twelve. The psychogenic seizures ceased with the onset of menstruation when she was 15, and instead, the patient developed heat sensations in her head, which became worse during menstruation. In addition, she suffered from constipation, meteorism, nausea, and developed a deep aversion to meat (Jung 1972, CW 2, § 793ff.). Numerous treatments remained unsuccessful. The patient could hardly sit. As a result, she spent most of the time walking to and fro in a restless manner, becoming increasingly idle, complaining and unsociable. When Jung first examined her, she had been ill for 17 years and was living at home. He diagnosed a chronic histrionic disorder with "*a complete subjugation of the personality by the illness*" (Jung 1972, CW 2, § 794).

Significant abnormalities in the first four word association tests (frequent responses using sounds, an abundance of errors, aborted tests, among others) indicated the patient's inability to engage in the experiment at all. Jung suspected that the young woman lacked the energy required for this and other tasks. Her libido was almost wholly lost in her symptomatology, leaving nothing for the external world. The aim of treatment was therefore to liberate the ego complex from the tyranny of the disease complex. But how could this be achieved? Jung presupposed that complexes are processed in dreams, which are then revealed to the consciousness in an unrecognizable and therefore, harmless form. He further assumed that complexes which influence associations in the awakened state and are revealed, among other things, in word association tests, also constellate in dreams (Jung 1972, CW 2, § 822).

Jung was therefore interested in the patient's dreams, in which the motifs of fire and blood initially predominated. She dreamed, e.g., about a room full of fire or blood. Because of the obvious connection between fire, blood and her sensations of heat, Jung said to the patient: "*Blood is red, red means love, fire is red and hot, surely you know the song: No fire, no coal can burn as hot, etc. Fire, too, means love* " (Jung, CW 2, § 823). This interpretation made such a strong emotional impression on the patient that she became highly embarrassed and broke out into uncontrollable laughter. No sooner had the subject of sexuality been voiced than other dream motifs appeared just a few days later. The room was now no longer filled with blood and fire, but full of cats or mice making a cacophony of noise. The patient associated this with the sound of mating cats which had disturbed her sleep at night over many years. A careful study of the associations which the noisy mice conjured up also revealed a connection with sexuality. Since all her other dreams were also about sexuality, Jung assumed that fear of sexuality, and thus a sexual complex, was at the bottom of the patient's illness.

A few weeks after treatment started, and around the same time as the new motifs of "cat" and "mouse" were emerging in ongoing dream interpretation, markedly altered association patterns became detectable in the fifth and sixth word association tests conducted. The nature of the associations, the decrease in the number of recall errors, as well as the patient's increased staying power showed that treatment was progressing. At the same time, the patient fell in love with Jung. By paying her attention, he became meaningful to her, and the greater part of her libido detached itself from her disease complex and started flowing towards him. Not only was she interested in him, but she also became less exhausted and significantly more active overall. The disease complex no longer had her completely in its grips because something had shifted on an energetic level. Libido in the sense of life force is etymologically synonymous with love, desire or hope in several languages. Such positive emotions are effective and have, as already mentioned, the power to change matter. Libido is capable of "liquifying" physical symptoms in the same sense as the alchemical "solve", even symptoms such as those that had become chronic in Jung's patient over the years.

However, the treatment failed, partly because the patient had to fund her own hospital treatment, as was customary at the beginning of the 20th century. Since she was poor, she was discharged early after only two months, and her dreams full of blood and fire returned, as well as the symptomatology existing before her hospitalization. Shortly before her discharge, Jung discovered references in her dreams to an experience she had had during pre-puberty which had triggered her illness. When asked more about this, the patient refused to confide in him further and declared that she was not able to discuss such an unpleasant sexual experience with him, but only with her mother (Jung 1972, CW 2, § 843). She was probably protecting herself emotionally, as she no longer had recourse to the therapy to deal with her traumatic experience.

According to Don Kalsched (Kalsched 2013), psychosomatic symptoms in particular are memory carriers of trauma – a thesis reflecting the results of the Adverse Childhood Experiences study (mentioned above in Subchapter 1.3 Psychoneuroimmunology – Stress, Emotion and the Immune System). Kalsched describes how early childhood trauma can cause the body's failure to connect adequately with the mind/psyche. In the face of unbearable experiences, the psyche resorts to a dissociative protective mechanism in which the ego distances itself from the body and seeks a safe refuge in mind and thought. In such cases, the body is insufficiently stimulated by emotions and functions merely as a kind of outer shell. At the same time, it becomes the bearer of traumatic scars which appear as physical symptoms in a compensatory manner and thus, cannot remain ignored in the long run (Kalsched 2013, 286f). The trauma sinks into and speaks through the body. Jung's patient's hot flashes, which she sought to cool down with cold washes, also repeatedly raised her awareness of her body. And her distended abdomen resembled a pregnant belly, thus also recalling her complexes around sexuality.

Generally speaking, however, repression, symptomatology, or an initially beneficial dissociation, among other things, are not permanent solutions, because whatever caused the trauma, i.e., the external abusers, remain unconsciously active as internal perpetrators or persecutors within the complexes.

4.2 Perpetrator and Victim as Complex Poles and their Significance for Psychosomatics

In our primary relationships, we constantly experience helplessness or powerlessness in the face of more mighty adults, who can either promote our self-efficacy and competencies or frighten, oppress, and threaten us. As weak children, we become victims because we experience adults as inhibitors, oppressors, or aggressors – more exactly, as perpetrators. The experiences we have of both sides of these relationships are stored in our complexes, which explains why in each of the latter, two poles are represented in our memory on a structural level, with an adult or perpetrator pole on the one hand, and a child or victim pole on the other. It may seem exaggerated to use the term perpetrator for the adult pole, but we are dealing first and foremost with activity, action, or aggression. In the original sense of the word, aggression means to move to a place, to go about, start or attack something, so aggression primarily involves energy, movement, and intention – all of which can be expressed in a loving or destructive way. The powerlessness experienced on the side of the child or victim pole also consists of a wide spectrum from appropriate to destructive helplessness, and from appropriate to destructive dependence.

The two complex poles are important for both our interpersonal relationships, as well as for psychosomatics. When the physician and psychoanalyst Michael Ermann (Ermann 2016, 373) refers to psychosomatoses as a resomatization of affective states, such as helplessness and hopelessness, then this implies that the victim pole in the complex is touched upon. The self-injury that borderline patients inflict upon themselves with the aim of being able to feel themselves physically can be understood from this point of view as an identification of the ego complex with the sadistic perpetrator pole. A self-injuring person activates the perpetrator pole at the moment of self-injury, acting in a self-effective, but unfortunately self-destructive way, so that the victim pole is experienced at the same time. Since many borderline patients were victims of violence and abuse in childhood, self-injury can also be interpreted as remembering and restaging acts of perpetration.

What does it take to overcome chronified victimization, for instance, in the form of a chronified psychosomatosis? "*You have to sacrifice the victim role, there is no way around it,*" is a central thesis to be found in the work of Verena Kast (Kast 1998, 98 (*translation from the German original*)). In the context of psychosomatic illness, this calls for not identifying with the victim pole, i.e., not allowing the victim identity to become set in stone, but rather recognizing and using existing spaces of freedom despite the illness. If people who are sick use the scope available to them and become able to allow their respective potential to take shape, then they draw on the self-efficacy, strength and resilience that are anchored in the child and adult poles. In this way, they are connected to self-resilience, and resilient people, in fact, do not identify with the victim role, instead using their resources to overcome stressful or overwhelming situations. Resilience is found at all ages: 80-year-old Frieda still lives in her own apartment. "Although I am becoming increasingly immobile due to my severe arthritis," she says, "I am still clear-headed, thank God. I need a lot of time for everyday things which have become very difficult to carry out. It takes me at least two hours to get dressed in the morning. In the afternoon, when my fingers are less stiff, I knit socks for my children and grandchildren." Neighbors and grandchildren enjoy being Frieda's guests and find solace in her composure and humor. Frieda focuses as much as possible on the things that she is still able to do. She does not allow her infirmity to dominate her life and refuses to see herself solely as a victim of her illness. Such an open-minded attitude is not at all easy to adopt, requiring recognition of and thankfulness for the little that is still possible despite the pain one feels. One should give as little attention and care as possible to suffering, as exemplified by the hero in the Grimm fairy tale "The Two Travelers" who takes this to heart. When his eye is gouged out, he remembers his mother's advice: "*Eat as much as you like and suffer what you must*" (Brothers Grimm 1946, 488). In other words, do not nurture suffering, or let it become overwhelming.

People who are able to follow this advice react differently on a physical level than people who cannot behave in this way, for whatever reason. Christian Schubert was able to demonstrate this in his "Life as it is Lived" studies. The majority of cancer patients, for example, are afraid of going for a check-up, as this constitutes a worrisome stress factor, which in turn can weaken the immune system and promote inflammation. Christian Schubert and his colleagues were therefore astonished to discover that a cancer patient reacted to an oncological check-up with a reduced inflammation level. Due to the fact that she had prepared for the examination in a very personal and creative way, she was doing well in a situation that many cancer patients experience as emotionally highly stressful. Self-care and self-efficacy, as well as the inner certainty of being up to the challenge proved to be the decisive factors (Schubert/Amberger 2019, 147f). These findings support Verena Kast's above-mentioned call to sacrifice the victim role and make use of one's breathing spaces in order to become healthier.

If chronically ill persons do not succeed in living up to the above principle, they run the risk of developing a victim identity, of falling prey to a disease around which everything else revolves. This can result in bitter feelings and tyranny towards the affected persons' immediate environment. If, in addition, they become convinced that absolutely no one can help them, they tend to take refuge in delusions of grandeur. Grandiose victims are convinced that their position is a particularly difficult one and, because their situation is particularly dire and there is no one competent enough to cure them, they exert great power. However, it is exactly this grandeur that fatally cements their victim status and consequently, their chronic illness. Neither inner nor outer resources can be mobilized and both therapists and physicians are left feeling increasingly helpless. Patients react with disappointment or resignation, occasionally criticizing or despising their therapist. Therapists slip towards the victim pole, as their normally effective professional skills – which represent the parent pole in the complex structure – are threatened, and they find this difficult to come to terms with. This explains why we tend to feel uneasy in the company of grandiosely sick people and sometimes even wish to be rid of them in order to avoid being pushed towards this unpleasant victim pole. Cord Benecke has since elaborated on how essential it can be for patients to have access to their helplessness and be able to admit this in an appropriate manner by simply saying "*I can be helpless*" (Benecke 2018, 27), which holds true not only for patients, but also for therapists. Facing one's own powerlessness or helplessness, enduring it, and dealing with it constructively is a therapeutic core competence when working with chronically or psychosomatically ill people.

However, emotions such as powerlessness, hopelessness or despair associated with the victim pole are not always directly observable, but hidden or repressed, for example, behind anger. Benecke therefore presented a five-stage emotion diagnosis to detect such repressed affects, and uses the example of a woman with depression to illustrate these steps. His patient was complaining in a monotonous, whining tone about her brother's lack of support in caring for their elderly parents, and about the way he was constantly blaming her (Benecke 2018, 21f).

In the first step to diagnosis, therapists admit without shame to their own immediate affective response to the patient's description. If this is to succeed, they must put aside professional posture and allow archaic human reactions to surface: "Am I feeling annoyed, irritated, impatient with anger, or...?" In the second step, therapists ask themselves how they would best like to deal with these affects. Should they just walk away, shake the patient, yell at them, or scold them? Again, it is important for them to shed inner "professional censorship" and perceive their archaic humanness. In the third step, therapists should ask themselves how the patient would feel if they gave in to such raw impulses, i.e., if they actually behaved as described in step two. The patient would probably feel exposed, rejected, abandoned, devastated, worthless or powerless. Benecke presupposes that the most intolerable affect has now been reached, which he refers to as the "core affect" which should generally be avoided. In the terminology presented above, this core affect belongs to the victim pole or child pole of the complex, namely the humiliated, abandoned, abused, or neglected child, to name just a few facets. The fourth step consists of questioning what the patient really desires and what her basic needs might be. She probably wants to be noticed and loved, and also seek recognition and justice. If therapists then observe, in the fifth step, the concrete behavior of the patient during the session – she accuses, demands, blames, is full of self-pity and self-righteousness – they need to circle back to the starting point of the diagnosis, because it is precisely this behavior that evoked the spontaneous affective response on the part of the therapist (Step 1). Tragically enough, the patient's behavior (Step 5) tends to bring about the opposite reaction (Step 2) to that which she probably desires (Step 4).

Benecke surmises that these extremely painful core affects often have to be repressed or compensated for with symptoms, aggression, hatred, lamentation, etc. (Benecke 2018, 70). Hence, they are not necessarily observable at first glance, but hidden beneath coping strategies or other protective mechanisms, as demonstrated by Christian Schubert's "Life as it is Lived" studies.

An emotionally stressful situation can weaken the immune system of a healthy person for short periods, whereas positive experiences and happiness have the opposite effect. Such ups and downs are part of a healthy life. However, counter patterns have also been observed in healthy people, meaning that – on an unconscious level – an actually pleasant experience can cause a physical stress reaction and weaken the immune system without the affected person noticing. This was the case in an apparently healthy young woman: Everyday positive emotional experiences strengthened her immune system, difficult ones weakened it, as expected. However, in one single instance, the opposite situation occurred, immunologically speaking, as pleasurable experiences with her partner weakened her immune system which responded as if under emotional stress (Schubert/Amberger 2019, 64f). Upon closer examination, it became apparent that a sore point in her unconscious, i.e., a complex and the associated core affect, had been touched upon and triggered this immune response. Internalized interpersonal experiences relating to her alcoholic father, the associated fears and ambivalent feelings played a significant role in this physical stress reaction.

Although unpleasant, it is necessary to penetrate through to these core affects in order to interrupt dysfunctional relational processes and the accompanying physical stress responses. It is here that not only unspeakable pain, but also a vital healing force can be found. From the point of view of Analytical Psychology, this vital force belongs to the positive child pole of our complexes, where not only experiences, such as helplessness, despair and the like, are stored, but also a positive archetypal core, which in the shape of the resilient, vital child – residing in all human beings – is repeatedly described in myths, fairy tales and lore. According to these, abused, threatened, or abandoned children have always existed and can be healed and go on to live full lives, which is why fairy tales are so important for children. Depriving them of fairy tales, most of which are cruel, also deprives them of the opportunity to learn not only how to survive the worst, but also how to be healed on a deeply spiritual level. Our ancestors' knowledge enriches the imagination and fosters hope. Instead of being repelled, what is frightful becomes the starting point of successful development processes. The Grimm fairy tales Snow White, Hans the Hedgehog, The Girl Without Hands, Cinderella, Hänsel and Gretel – to name just a few – show how children free themselves from existential threats and distress. Harry Potter is a modern fairy tale which has proved so successful worldwide because it takes up the archetypal theme of the orphaned child threatened by evil forces, and presents successful survival strategies. Children in fairy tales exhibit heroic, sometimes mischievous, or clever behavior in times of need and usually encounter numerous helpers along their difficult journeys. Because fairy-tale parents themselves often pose a threat, or at least are unable to help, children have to develop courage and creativity, as well as learn to take decisions and responsibility.

4.3 The Importance of Play and why it Matters

Back in real life, these skills are primarily acquired during childhood in play, namely free, spontaneous, physical play, which also includes roughhousing with other children. Panksepp was able to prove that in both mammals and children this form of play is anchored in the subcortical brain structures as an instinctive drive. Inherited from our ancestors, it represents an archeological treasure (Panksepp & Biven 2012, X), which is why it has archetypal quality from the perspective of Analytical Psychology. Unjustly, in the Western world, children are no longer allowed this type of PLAY, a so-called basic emotion, and its importance is devalued. However, the benefits of this archaic play for children are so extensive that Panksepp suggests prescribing a daily portion of "play diet" or even providing them with "sacred play refuges" (Panksepp & Biven 2012, 385f). What could the reasons for this be?

First, this type of play has an important social component, as children learn with whom they can cooperate and with whom maybe not. They experience competition, hierarchy, and friendship, and learn what it means to win or lose. Even if play ends in tears or frustration, the normal, healthy child is not dissuaded from playing again and again, as the fun factor prevails. The mutual joy, the shared laughter and good physical experience motivate them to continue playing. The PLAY system is the evolutionary source of mutual joy and laughter, and strengthens children's self-efficacy, their capacity for empathy, autonomy development, and the acquisition of skills to deal with unexpected events. It also promotes a sense of happiness and affirmation of life (Panksepp & Biven 2012, 365). Physical play thus has many positive aspects, although it is risky and dangerous. This distinguishes it from higher forms of play with differentiated, fixed rules. PLAY is quasi wild and uncivilized, and cognitively higher secondary and tertiary forms of play develop from it. Since extensive, daily play significantly reduces the symptoms of ADHD, Panksepp fears that prescribing Ritalin, which has been known to weaken the PLAY system, will hinder and damage the personality development of children affected by ADHD. Indeed, unrestricted physical play has been shown to have positive epigenetic effects on the higher cortical structures (Panksepp & Biven 2012, 379), as was demonstrated in rats. The positive social experiences of tickling and laughing in play caused new neurons to sprout in the hippocampus (Panksepp & Biven, 2012, XIIf). Since degenerative processes in the hippocampus can occur in severely depressed patients, the question arises whether such regeneration processes are also possible in humans. If this were to be the case, turning to play, to the "inner child gifted with play," could prove beneficial.

However, many adults greet this idea with skepticism or judge it as an imposition, including Jung himself. In 1913, when he was going through a period of strong inner pressure, and was feeling increasingly disoriented and helpless, he all of a sudden recalled a game he had been passionate about and played with great zeal as a child aged 11. It involved the building of a multitude of small castles and houses out of stones and clay, and Jung realized that he would only regain his creative vitality were he to take up this naive play again. However, he felt humiliated by the idea of returning to this activity at the age of 38 and hesitated for a long time, debating with himself before taking action. He finally ventured to do so, and began collecting stones after lunch or in the evenings, suitable for the construction of little houses, as he had done in his childhood. He experienced this play as emotionally beneficial, it cleared his thoughts and allowed his fantasies to flow freely again (Jaffé 1973, 173ff). Jung's activity had now become a cultivated form of play, i.e., was no longer instinctive primary PLAY, although still close to it in that it was spontaneous, without fixed rules, and emphatically physical by involving touching, fingering, and building. Touch or being touched are in fact essential factors in the PLAY system, with the sense of touch being the most important sensory modality of all, especially touch of the neck and chest area which awakens the archaic play instinct in mammals and humans. Bodily experience and sensuality are thus essential to this instinctual need. As with all instincts, the unconscious takes over and the ego merely executes the prescribed program. In animals, such instinctive action is an established process, but humans are natural and cultural beings. Based on our inherited primary-process instinctual disposition, we develop multi-layered emotions, differentiated cognitive abilities and control options – secondary and tertiary processes which are anchored in higher cortical structures. This is useful, because in our complex human world, instinctual behavior is not always helpful. Peter Fonagy's concept of mentalized affectivity describes this requisite human ability of regulating affects, defined as perceiving one's own affects, exploring, and withstanding them. In this context, overcoming the compulsion to act on affects impulsively is meant, and while affects are not completely repressed, they are deprived of some of their power (Fonagy, Gergely, Jurist & Target 2002). The ego thus gains a degree of freedom, which is a significant cultural achievement. In this day and age, however, the tension existing between instinct and culture harbors an increased risk of neglecting basic instinctual needs, such as getting sufficient sleep and having enough time for eating. In some people, over-evaluation of the intellect, performance, or efficiency results in a complete atrophy of natural human instincts.

This is another reason why including the body in therapy is becoming increasingly important, for example in the form of sandplay therapy, a psychosomatic method which allows patients to use sand to reproduce their emerging phantasies. Adults come into contact with a material that they probably enjoyed using in infancy, and which now helps them to replicate inner images in solid form. To this day, children love building sand pies and sandcastles. Sandplay allows adults to revisit this childlike creativity, and to speak with their hands as they did in the past. Ruth Ammann assumes (as did Broom and Whitmont, Chapter 1.1, C.G. Jung's Word Association Studies – Emotion, Imagination and Body) that we can only perceive and express body consciousness through the body, be it through dance, movement, intimate touch or just play. Especially in cases where psychosomatically or physically ill people have no words to express their symptoms, emotions or memories, their hands can form a bridge to what they are trying to say. This was exactly the case for one of Ruth Ammann's patients, a terminally ill 39-year-old woman. In adulthood, she was diagnosed with inherited progressive muscular dystrophy. Having witnessed the physical deterioration of her grandfather and mother, she knew what lay ahead of her and went into an overwhelming state of shock (Ammann 2019, 195). However, using sand as a medium enabled her to "speak," to represent and comprehend her sick body, and ultimately reach her muscle cells in a creative way. While she initially depicted her body as injured, suffering, riddled with holes, monstrous or ape-like, and was plagued with despair and feelings of inferiority, cell-like formations later appeared in the sand which she was able to nourish with food and energy, symbolized in the sand by small plates, glass stones or sun symbols. At the same time, she started to care for her sick body in the real world. Gaining this inner-soul attitude over a period of six years of sandplay was accompanied by an astonishing slowdown in the clinical progression of her disease (Ammann 2019, 210). Again, this experience proves how the most severe physical symptoms can be changed through mental work. It would appear important that a balance between light and dark forces is achieved in the process. During the patient's sandplay, the threatening figures of monster and monkey did not disappear entirely, but were put into a new context. In addition to the bad, there were the helpful, and in addition to the destructive, there were also the constructive aspects, leading the patient to remark: "*My illness will always be there, but the joy of life keeps it at bay*" (Ammann 2019, 213). In other words, the patient no longer saw herself solely as a victim of her illness, and was also able to perceive livability and allow herself the view that life was worth living. The disease had lost its power and the ego had regained a measure of freedom.

4.4 The Therapist's Body

During the course of the sandplay therapy carried out with the woman suffering from muscular dystrophy, Ruth Ammann occasionally felt her patient's pain in her own body (Ammann 2019, 205). She understands this as a resonance phenomenon akin to the vibration of musical instruments. If you pick up a violin and start to play, you will notice that the strings of another violin lying nearby also begin to reverberate.

Resonance is, in a sense, a response in the form of a vibration. The pain resonance Ruth Ammann refers to is called sympathetic pain memory by Thomas Fuchs (Fuchs 2008, 76). As a human phenomenon, this can also occur outside of therapy, for example, when someone witnesses the pain of a person close to them as a helpless bystander and then goes on to develop exactly the same symptoms in the same part of the body at the same time or a little while later. In ethnology and the psychology of religion, such phenomena have been known for a long time. For example, Elias Canetti (Canetti 1984, 337ff) describes a bushman who feels the strap of the sling in which his wife carries their child on his own shoulder. Another bushman feels pain in his body in the exact same spot where his father was wounded in the past. Every time his father plans a visit, this pain manifests itself a short while before his appearance, giving his body a sort of foreknowledge or announcement of his coming. In this particular example, physical resonance is temporally and spatially extended.

If we stick to the image of the resonating violins, physical symptoms can be regarded as "contagious" or transmissible, as it were. However, in connection with the therapeutic process, such resonance is possible in the therapist as well as in the patient. The "sick" as well as the "healthy" vibrations of the therapist can find resonance in the patient, thereby making health transferrable.

Therapists can use the physical symptoms they experience whilst treating patients in a variety of ways. On one occasion, when a patient was recounting a dream about flying which gave her pleasant feelings of freedom, her therapist suddenly felt a strange, painful pressure on his chest. As he could not find an explanation for or identify a personal link to this pressure, he asked the dreamer whether she had noticed a tension or tightness in her chest area. Almost immediately, she recalled the bad asthma attacks she had had during her childhood and the bitter conflicts with her controlling mother. At the time, she had managed to gain a feeling of freedom and security only by escaping into a phantasy world. Although she had not suffered from asthma again for a long time, she recognized that she still felt controlled and restricted in certain contexts, with no way of dealing with this on a constructive level. Instead, she took refuge in wishful thinking and phantasies, as she had done in the days of her childhood. Her therapist's physical symptom enabled the dreamer to realize that there was a connection between asthma – constriction – control – and escape into phantasy worlds (Whitmont & Perera 1989, 44).

It is therefore worth paying attention to one's body as a therapist as it sometimes knows exactly what the right thing to do is (Austin 2016b, 427), such as instinctively knowing what to say or what to leave unsaid, which posture is appropriate at a given moment and which is not. For example, I have twice found myself trying to avoid shaking hands when greeting persons. Although I overcame my physical reluctance and resisted this "impoliteness", I kept tabs on this strange impulse, which remained a mystery to me for a very long time. Initially, there was no reason to reject, fear, or distrust these persons, as inner images failed to appear, and no obvious reasons were discernable in outer reality. On each occasion, it took a few months before something very destructive came to light and my body had probably recognized this from the outset and sought to distance itself.

Also of relevance from a diagnostic point of view were the burning eyes which I developed during the second session with one of my patients, which was so painful and unpleasant that keeping my eyes open required the greatest of efforts. At the same time, my whole body began to feel more and more heavy, and I was hit with such extreme fatigue that it was exhausting to stay awake. I felt that I would faint at any moment. After bidding my patient goodbye, it took me only a few minutes to recover fully. This experience repeated itself twice before the patient underwent psychotic decompensation. When these same symptoms of physical somatic countertransference later came on with other patients, I knew we were approaching a psychotic aspect. Interestingly, Susan Austin described a very similar experience. She, too, could barely stay awake and complained of distorted vision during a patient's psychotic episode (Austin 2016a, 32).

If we understand psychosis as an "attack" on the ego complex and the capacity for consciousness, then fatigue and eye complaints are consistent phenomena. Nevertheless, the two physical experiences cannot be generalized, because each of us reacts very differently based on our subjective bodily experience and our complexes. If I start to freeze, my breathing becomes shallow or I become physically restless; I keep this under close observation and pay attention to inner images, then ask patients to likewise pay attention to their bodies and any images or feelings that may arise. Once I asked a patient to focus on her right hand after feeling multiple pain in my own right hand. Several sessions later, distant memories surfaced of her mother bandaging her right hand to prevent her from sucking her thumb.

4.5 Dreams and the Body

Back in their day, the Greek physicians Hippocrates and Galen were convinced of the diagnostic and prognostic value of dreams in mental and physical illness. Similarly, Jung also described how dreams can contribute to distinguishing functional and somatic symptoms in differential diagnostics. On one occasion, he was consulted by doctors who were mystified as to whether a 17-year-old girl was suffering from histrionic disorder or muscular dystrophy. After carrying out both a physical and psychological examination, Jung was also no further forward with a diagnosis, so he asked the young woman about her dreams. She recalled two recent nightmares, relating the first one as follows:

> *I am coming home at night. Everything is as quite as death. The door into the living room is half open, and I see my mother hanging from the chandelier, swinging to and fro in the cold wind that blows in through the open windows.*
> Another time she dreamt *that a terrible noise breaks out in the house at night. I get up and discover that a frightened horse is tearing through the rooms. At last it finds the door into the hall, and jumps through the hall window from the fourth floor into the street below. I was terrified when I saw it lying there, all mangled.* (Jung 1985, CW 16 § 343).

The dream ego witnesses two suicides that occur during the night and observes what happens behind the scenes in secret. In this respect, the ego gains access to knowledge of the unconscious. The central dream motifs are *mother* and *horse*, so the question arises as to what extent the meaning of the two symbols overlaps. As an archetype, the mother encompasses everything natural and living. She is the great weaver, creating the material, the matter, and hence, the body with its unconscious vegetative functions, to name just a few facets. The horse symbolizes the animalistic, which bears the rider and, in this way, the human ego or ego complex. It often represents physical drives and the associated vital energies. As a matter of fact, muscular dystrophy is a genetic destruction program and, as it represents the degeneration of muscle cells, it is an autonomously occurring natural process. Both dreams present images of the self-destruction of vegetative and animal life, which corresponds to the physiological processes of muscular dystrophy. Since cellular physiology forms the basis of individual life, physical death inevitably means the death of the whole human being, for there is no earthly life without a body. And as in the patient's dreams, the conscious ego must also watch and endure these physiological processes of destruction in the waking world. Therefore, based on these dream images, Jung became certain that the dreamer was suffering from an organic disease with a lethal outcome, which was later confirmed. The two dreams are thus very exact in the images that were selected, as it is not the conscious ego of the young woman which dies first, but physical life.

In this respect, Mother Nature is not exclusively benevolent in that she both gives and takes life. Symbolically speaking, birth and death are in her hands – she is the mother of life and the mother of death. This symbolism became significant for a young woman who was feeling very miserable about her unintended pregnancy. Immediately after she dreamt that *her mother tore out a blooming rosebush by its roots*, she miscarried (Whitmont 1993, 117). In this dream, the mother acts as the Death Mother, destroying life – in this case plant life – along with all its roots. Viewed from the outside, the unborn child in its early stages is indeed primarily vegetative life, but is represented in the dream as something complete in the form of a blossoming rose. According to the language of dreams, this spontaneous abortion does not merely cause the loss of a slimy and bloody clump of cells, but of a flower, which is a metaphor for love in many cultures. Although the child was unwanted, the dream places the unborn life in the context of a collective symbol of love, either because there might have been an opportunity for the mother to ultimately become capable of bestowing love, contrary to her expectations, or on the other hand to be loved by her child.

If one wishes to follow the above interpretation, the pregnant woman's dream indicated a future event. This predictive dream quality was experienced by another young woman who developed encephalitis after a tick bite. After the acute high-fever phase of the illness had subsided, the patient continued to suffer from strong, prolonged, and very debilitating tremors in her head and one arm which were triggered by loud noises, physical exertion, or excitement. This worried the patient greatly, especially since a computed tomography (CT) scan revealed a small lesion in her brain. The doctors could not tell her whether these uncontrollable tremors would ever cease. The patient was desperate, because she could no longer enjoy the carefree life she had had before the infection. She feared that she would lose her mind and go crazy. One afternoon, after the patient had fallen asleep thoroughly exhausted by her strong tremors, the following dream transpired: "I am lying on the sofa in the living room. Suddenly, I hear the sound of a strong wind coming through an open window. The wind is powerfully swinging tall trees in the garden. Then, I hear a voice "don't worry, the wind is making them shake, it's not your head."

Upon awakening, the dreamer realized that the storm had not raged in the garden, but in her dream, and knew instantly that she would not go mad. Although the storm was strong enough to cause living things to sway – comparable to trembling – she knew with certainty that it would eventually ease. At that point, the trees in her dream would no longer shake, and analogously, her trembling would disappear. Reassured by these images, the dreamer recovered step by step. In fact, six months later, the tremors would occur only after times of extreme stress and then last no more than a minute or two.

A similar temporal relationship between physical symptoms and dreams was also observed by psychiatrist and analyst Alfred Ziegler. Whenever a patient exhibiting typical physical complaints awakens from a dream which they remember, Ziegler refers to this as a pathognomonic dream and goes on to suggest that dream images provide a commentary on physical symptoms, and thus reveal an interconnectivity between the mental and physical level. He describes the case of a 41-year-old humanities scholar who awakens during an asthma attack *and recalls that he dreamed he was suspected of having committed murder, since everywhere he had been, bodies have been discovered. He therefore suggests that the police accompany him and guard him day and night to convince them that he has nothing to do with these deaths. As the surveillance begins, the earth begins to tremble, his feet start to slide, dust and dirt swirl in the air, and the dreamer sinks down, deeper and deeper. The earth begins to cover him, and he begins to scream* (Ziegler 2000, 55).

As the dream ends, the air is full of dust and stones, making it hard to breathe easily – which is exactly what asthma sufferers have to deal with. The images in the dream describe a very personal trigger situation: the shortness of breath is connected to the dreamer's intention to prove his innocence. His request to be monitored by the authorities in order to prove his "clean slate", is the trigger for the air pollution and the ensuing asthma attack. This was preceded by the interest in the murder shadow manifested in the dream, i.e., the question whether the dreamer had killed something living, something human, within himself – something completely unimaginable for the dreamer, as he is totally convinced of his own integrity and righteousness. But from the point of view of the unconscious, this personal shadow theme is linked to his asthma.

A young woman suffering from severe arthritis was also made aware of an important individual shadow theme by means of a dream. She awoke with a terrible pain in her wrist and recalled dreaming that *she is in a large room where a large number of people are seated at tables, waiting for something to eat. The young woman is the only one working and has to serve the guests and lift heavy pitchers to pour drinks into their glasses. A grinning man blackmails her by forcing her to do so* (Ziegler 2000, 107f). In her dream, the dreamer is portrayed as a hard-working waitress. She does not do this out of pleasure or because it is her profession, but because she submits to a man's command. Accordingly, a male authority seems to be at work in her, compelling her to serve others. In the dream, she is not free and she does not dare to complain that the work is too much for her, that she would be glad of help or that she does not want to continue anymore. However, in the waking world, it is her arthritis that frees her from these duties, which she can no longer carry out in real life, but can master in her dreams, albeit reluctantly. This comes at a high price, though, because arthritis also robs her of freedom in many other areas of life. Her body thus not only inhibits her ability to work, but also denies her pleasurable experiences and personal scope.

The unconscious therefore repeatedly links mental and physical reality by providing images which aid diagnosis and prognosis. This was also true in the case of a woman suffering from cancer, who tormented herself with questions about why she of all people had developed this disease. She was convinced that she had done something wrong, or that she had committed a crime for such an illness does not come out of the blue. Unable to find a valid explanation, she began to feel increasingly desperate. Then she had a dream: "*I am in a lovely place. Suddenly, a heavy thunderstorm brews up. I see three birch trees, and lightning strikes the middle one. I discover that this kind of thing happens often.*" In contrast to the two dreams discussed earlier, this one has nothing to do with personal shadow aspects, but with the dreamer's observation of natural phenomena. Due to the force of lightning, a birch tree breaks in two, burns, chars, and dies. As a widespread and multilayered symbol, the tree also stands for vegetative life, which is firmly anchored in the earth, striving heavenward. In this way, the tree resembles a human being who goes through a mental-spiritual development, while remaining rooted in the body. And just as an individual tree can die for no particular reason, a human being can die without having done anything wrong. Lightning, seen as a tool of the gods in ancient Germanic and Greek mythology, is a transpersonal natural force that knows no moral standards. For the dreamer, these images were terrible and at the same time, extremely liberating. She was able to overcome her brooding compulsion because there was no explanation for the lightning strike – fate can simply be cruel and unjust. Moreover, Golgotha came to mind, the hill where Christ was crucified, on the middle one of three wooden crosses. Here, three trees had become trees of death, and she could relate somewhat to the meaning of "My God, my God, why hast thou forsaken me." She felt guiltless and unprotected, also abandoned and yet, not completely alone, because she suspected that she was not the only one who had to go through such an experience.

The dream a woman had in which she *sees her house roof pierced by the branches of a tree torn loose in a windstorm* (Whitmont & Perera 1989, 138) also illustrates natural destruction with no human involvement or cause. If we think of the house as a symbolic representation of the body, then the head, as the uppermost part has been hit. Indeed, a day later, the dreamer suffered from a stroke. This physical event can only be linked to the dream in retrospect, since it is never fully clear whether images in a dream relate to an inner mental, or a concrete external, physical reality.

The following two dreams feature a cat attacking the dream ego, and in each case, the attack takes place on the very organ that is diseased:

A woman suffering for months from weeping eczema of her right breast underwent a trial excision and afterwards dreamed: "*I am walking through a forest, when a wild cat suddenly jumps on me and scratches my right breast. It bleeds and is very painful. The cat runs away.*" A few days later, she was diagnosed with breast cancer. Another profoundly religious woman dreamed about *hesitating to take a picture of the Virgin Mary off the wall, even though it no longer matches her home decor. As a result, she is bitten in the abdomen by her cat.* The dream preceded acute diverticulitis (Whitmont 1993, 118). Being freedom-loving creatures, cats do not really allow humans to train them. Whenever they are hungry or want to be petted, they try to draw attention to themselves until their needs and picky eating habits are satisfied. This penchant for pleasure and right to a self-determined existence may have contributed to their demonization and vilification as companions of witches from the Middle Ages onwards. In those days, women, who like cats, tried to preserve a certain degree of self-will and independence instead of subordinating themselves to patriarchal structures and male demands, were denounced as witches. In both the above dreams, the instinctive female aspect led to self-destructive action and questions about how the patients had embraced their femininity up until that moment.

The above examples illustrate that symbols, especially those denoting nature, the weather, animals, or plants can point to physical phenomena. This is again taken up in the following dream published by Marie-Louise von Franz (von Franz 1986, 78), which a 52-year-old, terminally ill man had:

> *I see a wood that is green, not yet autumnal. A fire is raging, which destroys it completely. It is a terrible sight. Afterwards, I am walking through the burned-up area. Everything has turned into black coal and ashes, but in the midst lies a boulder of red stone. It shows no trace of the fire, and the thought that the fire has not even touched or blackened it fills me with intense joy.*

As far as age was concerned, the patient was indeed not yet in the autumn of life, but knew that he would die prematurely. The dream image of a forest destroyed by fire is a metaphorical description of the destruction of the vegetative life of the human body. Yet, the dream ego was able to perceive that the destruction was not total and that a special stone remained completely undamaged. There is a transient and enduring presence, which is why von Franz suspected this dream suggests the continuation of life after death, for the unconscious seems to believe in this concept (von Franz 1986, IX). Skeptics will object that this is only wishful dreaming. However, many analysts see dreams as a mostly natural mental event, uninfluenced by the ego's wishes. And the sometimes brutal or compassionless images with which the end of physical life is addressed contradict the notion that dreams are merely of a wish-fulfilling character, as exemplified by the dream of a seriously ill woman: "*I meet my husband, who tells me everything will be all right, and that I need not worry. Then I bid him goodbye and find myself at the seashore. The beach is lonely and the light darkening. The shore is empty except for some barges.*" The patient described her husband as a foolish optimist, unable to face reality, and comprehended that the ferry to the other shore – an ancient mythological motif – was waiting to take her on her final journey to the afterlife (Whitmont & Perera 1989,

132f). Nothing was glossed over, nor anything dramatized in this dream.

In another dream (von Franz 1986, 30), a man trying to cope with his impending death *perceives the moan of a chainsaw and the crack of falling trees as he is walking through a forest in winter. Suddenly the dreamer finds himself once more in a forest, but higher up as it were. There he meets his long-dead father, who tells him he should no longer be concerned about the trees being hewed down below, now that they are both in a different forest.* In this dream, death appears as a woodcutter, which resembles medieval images depicting death as a reaper with a scythe, who cuts down vegetative life – a symbol of the mortal body. However, on a higher level, there is another forest, which could not only suggest the immortality of the soul, but also the Christian idea of the resurrection of the body and reunion with those who have gone before. Such images can comfort the seriously ill, as a young woman confirmed shortly before her death. She dreamed: *"I am walking in my garden. It is cold and foggy. I feel frightened, all the plants have been eaten away and I see the bare earth. Suddenly a voice speaks: Don't forget the lily bulbs under the earth, they remain undamaged and will bloom again next summer."* Despite the destruction of the plants above the ground, the bulbs hidden in the dark guarantee that in due time, life will sprout anew. Birth and death are cyclical phenomena on the border between visible and invisible life.

5.

Cancer as a Disease

5.1 Fearing Cancer

"My children now know that I won't die of breast cancer," wrote 37-year-old actress and filmmaker Angelina Jolie after her double-sided mastectomy in 2013. She had undergone this radical procedure to reduce her genetic risk of breast cancer from about 87% to just under 5%. Her mother, grandmother and aunt had all died of breast or ovarian cancer, respectively, and she wanted to prevent contracting the disease at all costs. Two years later, she also had her ovaries removed after a first growth of malignant cells was suspected (Stockrahm 2015). Like Angelina Jolie, a great many people fear cancer, which has even been described by scientists as "the emperor of all maladies, the king of terrors" (Mukherjee 2010, xviii, 21). These metaphorical images are in tune with the fear and fright that a cancer diagnosis can cause – a fear that is significant because current evidence suggests it has a major impact on the progression of cancer. Clinical trials show, for example, that if breast cancer patients with high blood pressure are treated with beta blockers, their risk of metastases decreases by 57%, and their risk of dying from breast cancer by 71%. This most likely relates to the fact that beta blockers, by inhibiting the activity of the sympathetic nervous system, can significantly reduce the scaring thoughts associated with cancer. Such drug-induced relaxation, along with the reduction of anxiety and distress, promotes healing processes (Schubert 2015, 94). These and other findings in psychoneuroimmunological research have led to the conclusion that anything that helps decrease a cancer patient's fear has a significant health-promoting effect. The treatment of anxiety is thus a very central factor.

What is it that frightens us about this disease? Although there are more than a hundred different diseases which run very different courses and have a varying probability of cure, all types of cancer have one characteristic in common, namely the autonomous, immoderate, and unstoppable cell growth, which is categorized as malignant. Cancer is the only disease which we associate with evil, and this can cause disturbing inner images and fearful emotions to surface. On the external level, it is the mortality rate that frightens us, because despite the increased probability of a cure, about 25% of all deaths in the Western world are ascribed to cancer, and about one in every two cancer patients still dies. But surgery, radiation, or chemotherapy cause discomfort and generate fear, and might occasionally force radical life changes. And last, but not least, the uncertainty as to whether the usually lengthy treatment will defeat the cancer or not is understandably frightening.

A retired registrar was overcome with high anxiety when a tumor recurrence was detected at the scar site of the breast-conserving surgery she had undergone after a breast cancer diagnosis two years earlier. Due to the recurrence, medical experts were of the unanimous opinion that breast amputation was unavoidable. At that moment, the patient was psychologically distressed and realized that she could not survive without her breast. She was beset with forgotten, painful experiences of loss, which her emotional reactions made her aware of. The patient, e.g., remembered that as a four-year-old girl, she had not been allowed to take her favorite book, which was very precious to her, back home with her when leaving the hospital after treatment. And a few months later, when fleeing at the end of World War II, she had been forced to leave her only, much loved toy behind. Many years later, one of her children only lived for a few months. The patient felt that she had never really come to terms with these and similar experiences of loss. Therefore, she accepted her fear of losing her breast as real and sought alternative methods of treatment to preserve it. Two days before going to consult her gynecologist, the following dream presented itself: "*I am about to be operated on. The surgeons are holding my breast in their hands. Horrified, I say: don't throw it into the garbage.*" She went to the scheduled appointment at her gynecologist's with a bad presentiment. When he read the medical reports she had brought with her, he strongly warned her against seeking breast-conserving surgery, which would be negligent and out of the question in her case. Upon hearing this, the patient burst into tears and the doctor explained that she must trust him, as he only wanted what was best for her and that there really was no alternative if she desired to be cured. However, the woman, as in her dream, could not bear the thought of the doctors throwing a part of herself, her breast, into the garbage as waste. She simply could not agree to mutilating her body although this was considered the optimum life-saving measure from a rational medical point of view. Being aware of the risks involved, she insisted on keeping her breast. She was grateful for having the option of deciding whether she should accept this fateful loss or not, and after careful deliberation, made her choice. By refusing surgery and listening to her emotions, she made what was the right decision for herself – which in turn greatly frightened her relatives.

As shown clearly in this example, fear of cancer takes a variety of extremely different forms. Whereas some people, such as Angelina Jolie, pursue every medical option available as a means towards conquering their fear of cancer, others, such as the above-mentioned patient, develop a fear of the consequences of medical treatment. It is not only patients themselves who must confront their fears, but also their relatives, doctors or therapists who must ultimately ask themselves how to deal with fear when their expectations do not coincide with those of the person affected by cancer. No patent remedy exists, but to my mind, paying close attention to one's emotions and inner images is essential, as well as initially allowing oneself feelings of annoyance and displeasure. Perhaps we will then accept that the person in question has to either follow their own path in order to stay true to themselves, or that they have become stuck in a complex which induces them to make unwise decisions. Such was the case of a 50-year-old engineer, who was being clinically treated for bone cancer and was having heated arguments about further treatment with his physicians, rejecting all the options proposed to him. The doctors were annoyed by his chronic dissatisfaction, his constant objections and reproaches to the point that they would have liked to be rid of him. Then, in the course of psycho-oncological therapy, the patient recounted a nightmare he had had about building himself a new house for which he had done the structural calculations, as well as managed and supervised the construction of the outer shell. When the structural work had been completed, a young engineer told him that it would collapse shortly because he, the dreamer, had made a mistake in his calculations and had given the bricklayers wrong instructions. The dreamer woke up in a great fright, as in all his professional life he had never before committed such an error.

Since only male figures featured in the patient's dream, concepts of male identity, his responsibilities and his father's image could be discussed with him. He realized that his deep aversion to his father had overshadowed the vast majority of his encounters with authority figures. Being trapped in this father complex, he demonstrated a fundamental tendency to reject and attack authority. And this complex-like rejection had also "poisoned" the relationship with his doctors. Stuck in a power struggle with his medical team, as he had once been with his father, he was not able to handle the treatment options available to him in a constructive manner.

5.2 Cancer as a Biological Phenomenon

What is cancer then anyway? By the mid-19th century, Rudolf Virchow had come to recognize that a cancerous tumor was not an independent entity within the organism. Every cancerous growth originates from a cell in the organism and forms a new type of tissue, which is why Virchow spoke of neoplasia. On average, about four million cells are formed in our body per second, meaning that from fertilization of the egg cell to death, an unimaginable 1000 trillion cell divisions take place in the course of a human lifetime. If we were to take a few cells of supporting tissue from our body and put them into a test tube, they would die after about 40-50 cell divisions. Their life span is therefore limited and today, we are familiar with some of the genes that are responsible for the cellular "switch-off" process that leads to a cell's aging and death. The key to the riddle of cell aging is to be found at the ends of the chromosomes, where so-called telomeres are located, which act as "protective caps" to shield the genetic material threaded onto the chromosomes. With each cell division, a tiny bit of the telomeres is lost until they are used up, at which point the cell dies. Unlike healthy "mortal" cells, however, cancer cells are able to turn on a gene that produces telomerase, an enzyme which prevents the degradation of the protective telomeres. Cancer cells have thus overcome the cellular control mechanisms of aging and dying, and are able to divide not only 40-50 times, but indefinitely. Cells from cancer growths can divide and multiply in test tubes even though the people from whom they were taken have already died, as in the case of Henrietta Lacks, who died of cervical cancer in 1951. Her cancer cells continue to multiply to this day in an American laboratory in Baltimore (Skloot 2011). In principle, cancer cells are immortal, but healthy germ cells and stem cells from the blood, the skin or bone marrow also possess this property. They stand ready for new life to develop and differentiate, and are not affected by gradual telomere loss either, because they, too, possess the protective enzyme telomerase. Germ and stem cells on the one hand, and cancer cells on the other are capable of dividing over and over again, showing that life-building and life-destroying cells have the same ability.

Today, we also know that the precursors of cancer-causing genes, so-called proto-oncogenes, play a key role in the development of a cancer cell. These proto-oncogenes are found in all healthy human cells, and smoking, nuclear radiation, asbestos, and many other factors can cause them to mutate into oncogenes, turning healthy cells into cancer cells after several preliminary modifications. This explains why smokers and non-smokers alike can get the same type of cancer, since smoking only increases the probability of mutation of the proto-oncogenes present in every human genome.

However, it takes many mutations for a cancer cell to develop, not only in proto-oncogenes, but also in tumor suppressor genes, also known as anti-oncogenes, which prevent excessive cell division or even induce cell death in case of severe genetic defects. If anti-oncogenes are switched off by mutation, while activated oncogenes are already present in a cell, the way is paved for this cell to divide and multiply, giving cancer a green light. The aforementioned incessant cell division and cell proliferation will then set in, leading to the growths that we know as tumors in most cancer forms.

5.3 Metaphorical Aspects of Cancer

When a pregnant woman begins to notice her baby bump, she is filled with joy, knowing that a new human is developing within her body. However, people are scared to death when they know that a tumor, not a baby, is growing inside of them. This was known as a "demonic pregnancy" in ancient times. A multiplying cancer cell does not create life, but destroys it, which is why we refer to it as "malignant". It divides even more frequently than a healthy cell and behaves autonomously, multiplying without regard for the law and order of healthy tissue. This means that cell proliferation is not only never-ending, but that the cancer cell has the ability to leave the original cell compound and pass through the barriers of blood vessels or other tissue with the help of suitable enzymes. A healthy cell cannot do this, because breaking away from its stem tissue means that it must perish. Cancer is invasive and transgressive in behavior. Unlike healthy tissue, a malignant tumor can migrate beyond the boundaries of the affected organ and establish itself in adjacent tissue.

Obviously, growth can either enable or destroy life, and while healthy and malignant growth are closely related on a genetic level, they are complete opposites (Mukherjee 2010, 6). Such opposites are repeatedly seen as the positive or negative pole of archetypal forces. As mentioned, the great Mother Earth not only continues to give life, nurture it, and make it grow, but keeps taking it away. If nothing were to die, there would be too little space for all of us, and growth would be stifling. It is nature itself that provides for the good of all by balancing life-giving and destructive forces. Such opposing forces always were and still are experienced as divine because they remain largely beyond the control of the ego. For this reason, we find the shared identity of such opposites in images of God. The Hindu god Shiva is, for example, depicted as a great dancer who creates the world through dance, only to destroy it again. Shiva thus symbolizes both the creative and the destructive forces of this world (von Glasenapp 1995, 33 ff).

This dichotomy of opposites supports the notion that cancer incorporates a religious, i.e., transpersonal dimension. Therefore, my thesis from the viewpoint of Analytical Psychology is that the destructive elements of cancer, which cause such great fear inside us, are a physical manifestation of the shadow side of the Self – the intrinsic, destructive side of divine creation. This is also evident in the fact that cancer can occur in both animals and plants. As a disease, it is a phenomenon immanent to creation, and as such, the acausal embodiment of the dark aspects of the Divine. This statement implies that ultimately, we do not really know why life is given only to be destroyed again. Primordial phenomena pre-exist which we can only partially control. This religious dimension is also reflected in the diction chosen by physicians, probably on an unconscious level. The American researcher Sidney Faber, e.g., spoke about his "crusade against cancer" back in the 1950s, and the American surgeon William Halsted, whose ultra-radical techniques in breast cancer surgery were seldom called into question until the 1970s, was called the "patron saint of cancer surgery" (Mukherjee 2010, 147).

As already discussed in the context of anorexia, a potential connection with both the Zeitgeist and collective values can also be assumed in the case of cancer. The characteristic hallmarks of a cancer cell are not limited to the disease, but in terms of phenomenology, also permeate various spheres of Western culture. One example is the dream of humanity to become older and older or even immortal, often in ignorance of the fact that we are more fragile and susceptible to disease in very old age. Aging itself harbors an increasing risk of cancer because the chance of genetic mutation likewise increases. The shadow aspects of the idea of human immortality must also be considered, as becoming immortal would be quite antisocial, coming at the expense of future generations and leaving no room for new life.

The quest for an autonomous life without limits or boundaries is also high on today's social agenda. As the Western world continues to strive for economic growth, we are faced with barely manageable mountains of garbage, overutilization, and environmental pollution. We have become increasingly and more painfully aware of these life-threatening shadow aspects of unbridled, excessive growth nowadays – which are likewise reflected in the suffering of cancer patients.

Exuberant growth is the theme of the Grimm fairy tale "Sweet Porridge" about a girl and her mother who had nothing left to eat:

> There was a poor but pious little girl who lived alone with her mother, and they no longer had anything to eat. So the child went into the forest, and there an old woman met her. She knew of the girl's sorrow, and presented her with a little pot, which when she said, "Little pot, cook," would cook good, sweet millet porridge, and when she said, " Little pot, stop," it stopped cooking. The girl took the pot home to her mother, and now they were freed from their poverty and hunger, and ate sweet porridge as often as they chose. One time when the girl had gone out, her mother said, "Little pot, cook." And it did cook, and she ate until she was full, and then she wanted the pot to stop cooking, but did not know the word. So it went on cooking and the porridge rose over the edge, and still it cooked on until the kitchen and whole house were full, and then the next house, and then the whole street, just as if it wanted to satisfy the hunger of the whole world. It was terrible, and no one knew how to stop it. At last, when only one single house remained, the child came home and just said, "Little pot, stop," and it stopped cooking, and anyone who wished to return to the town had to eat his way back. (Brothers Grimm 1946, 372)

Something similar is described in Goethe's poem "The Sorcerer's Apprentice", when, during the absence of the old wizard, the sorcerer's apprentice utters the words he learned from his master to enchant the broom to carry water for him. Suddenly he realizes that the words needed to stop the broom from fetching water have slipped his mind, and he is faced with a terrifying flood. In the moment of his greatest distress, the old master, who knows the correct words to put the broom in its place, returns and can thus end the flood.

Human interaction with the forces of nature is the theme addressed in both the fairy tale and the poem. Thanks to our knowledge and cultural achievements, we are no longer completely at the mercy of nature, having learned to harness natural resources to our benefit. If we were to follow the two stories above, however, it is imperative that we are not only able to initiate, but also to halt processes again, which is the bottom line of both texts. As soon as humans intervene in a process, they need to be in control of both the beginning and the end in order to prevent destructive growth. In relation to cancer, this can be understood as a summons to pay closer attention to the factors that have been shown to cause the disease. For example, we know many substances are carcinogenic, but this does not stop us from using them, either for the sake of convenience or profit. As humans, we must ultimately bear responsibility, but it is important to be aware that we are only partially responsible, namely for what we ourselves initiate. Cancer is an age-old natural phenomenon, as evidenced in ancient Egyptian mummy and Stone Age skeleton finds. It has always existed and always will, even though it has been demystified of some of its horror.

Filmmaker Susan Sontag was vehemently opposed to this kind of metaphorical approach to illness, convinced that the healthiest way to be sick is to completely disengage oneself from metaphors (Sontag 1978, 3), because the sick are at risk of being stigmatized, blamed or marginalized by such imagery. This may be true, but in my opinion, we cannot completely prevent the projection of images onto a disease. They may, but need not necessarily, lead to dysfunctional behavior patterns, because the images relate primarily to the disease itself and not to the patient. Hence, metaphors are not simply false, but may rather refer to something intrinsic and hidden about the disease. This also explains why images change in the collective consciousness once we know more about a disease and better treatment options are available. The uncanny and mysterious recede into the background, especially when an even more threatening and unknown disease comes into the focus of public attention. The metaphors described by Susan Sontag 40 years ago have thus also changed to some extent.

One problematic tendency still in existence today is that of relating certain diseases to the traits of those affected. For a long time, tuberculosis was considered to be a disease associated with distinguished, sensitive and delicate people in Central Europe. Moreover, it was linked with sadness and creativity (Sontag 1978, 28ff). Thus, in some social circles, tuberculosis had a positive nimbus which we would nowadays consider as rather disconcerting. This demonstrates how attributions can change over time, and even in the case of cancer, connections between personality structure and disease are still under discussion today. The suppression of feelings, a tendency towards self-punishment or a reduced ability to feel joy are, in particular, thought to be trigger factors. However, recent epidemiological studies cannot conclusively prove that psychological factors cause cancer. In view of what is known about the biology of cancer in our day, such a monocausal stance is untenable, as only the complex interplay of genetics, environmental factors, lifestyle, and other aspects can cause cancer to develop. Still, data relating to the risk of cancer recurrence and the impact of psychological stressors is more consistent. Hopelessness and the suppression of feelings are prognostically unfavorable stressors (Schubert 2015c, 89). These findings are relevant to the physical effects of psychotherapeutic treatment, as pointed out by psychoneuroimmunologist Kurt Zänker, who notes that "language is epigenetics." What he means is that according to current knowledge, the gene mutations responsible for the development of cancer do not represent an irrevocable fate. Whether genes are switched on or off is determined by the methyl groups located on these genes, which are in charge of genetic activation and deactivation. Because these methyl groups with their control function are virtually *on top* of the genes, we speak of *epi*genetics. When constructive, meaningful conversations are held – such as in psychotherapy – neuroimmunological processes are triggered that have an effect on the innermost cell nuclei and their epigenetically active structures. Language has an influence on the activation and deactivation of genes, and stress-relieving conversations, positive experiences and encounters reduce the risk of disease or relapse (Schubert/Amberger 2019, 157).

5.4 The Word Cancer and its Symbolic Context

It is worth taking a look at the etymological root of the name of a disease if one takes this as a condensed version of its history with a kernel of truth hidden behind its symbolic aspects. The word "cancer" (carcinoma) is said to have been coined by Hippocrates (460 BC), as the swollen vessels of breast cancer supposedly reminded him of the limbs of a crab. What we refer to as the "end stages" of breast cancer was often visible in former times, with the dark red, coarse, ulcerating growths, which disfigure a person's breast. This resembled a crustacean, specifically the hermit crab, which was thought of as a bringer of bad luck in ancient times because of its backward movements.

This eponym has several characteristic features which afford a glimpse into the symbolism of cancer: two are mythological (the antagonism between the crab and the hero Heracles, and the link to the pre-Olympic goddess Medusa), and two are biological (the impregnable hard shell and the need for a periodic shell change) (Daniel 2017, 126f).

Greek mythology describes how the crab Karkinos seizes and bites the foot of the extremely strong, highly victorious hero Heracles and halts his progress towards battle with the Lernaean serpent. The goddess Hera takes great pleasure in the fact that Heracles has been impeded in this way and, to express her gratitude for this deed, places the crab among the starry skies. Ever since, the sun enters the zodiac sign of Cancer on the summer solstice in the Northern Hemisphere to begin its retreat, with the days gradually becoming shorter and darker.

If we take this mythical image as a symbol for cancer, then it follows that the disease has the power to hinder those who are affected from continuing their previous social progress and striving for success. In some circumstances, sick individuals are even forced to go into "reverse gear", a fact confirmed by sufferers who normally have to take it easy for many months, restricting themselves, and refraining from outside activities. Treatment is usually lengthy which means that delivering at peak performance is seldom possible. In some cases, a person may have already passed the zenith of their career and their current position in the meritocracy is challenged. One may argue that people can also be forced out of social performance by other severe chronic diseases, which is certainly true, and the above is not entirely exclusive to cancer. However, different illnesses are associated with different images, as in the case of a heart attack, which is often linked to the image of busy, performance-oriented people. Since performance is highly respected in the Western world, heart attacks also have a rather good image, which cancer does not have, even though the disease no longer has to be kept secret, as was still the practice a few decades ago. Cancer is exceptional, not least because there are often no symptoms at all or only mild, non-specific ones at the time of diagnosis. In terms of symptoms, people often go to hospital feeling quite healthy only to leave feeling much worse, which tends to be the other way around with other illnesses. The physical and mental suffering of cancer patients and the associated limitations, such as hair loss, vomiting, extreme weakness or even the creation of an artificial bowel outlet, often begin with treatment. Patients naturally hope that these symptoms are only transitory and the suffering temporary, but a lot of rest and retreat from habitual activities is still required. When the worst side effects have been overcome to the extent where patients would like to and are able to return to work, they often fail to regain their former level of performance, as long-term follow-up treatment with anti-hormones in particular quite often leads to exhaustion, joint pain or inflammation. This puts a strain not only on the cancer patients themselves, but also on colleagues who might have good-naturedly managed the workload amongst themselves over a period of several months, hoping that their sick team-mate would come back completely healed. Should this turn out not to be the case, there is the danger that colleagues might no longer display the same level of empathy and acceptance. Upon their return to work, the patient's exhaustion and associated limitations could well be met with anger, dismissal, or reproach.

A darker feature of cancer is reflected in the image of the Greek goddess Medusa, who was depicted in ancient times on coins and clay bowls as having the face of a crustacean. Medusa is a monstrous, terrifying, ancient goddess with a head of hair consisting of snakes, and anyone who dared to look at her was turned to stone. This image resonates with the first reaction which sufferers or their relatives have upon receiving a cancer diagnosis – they feel petrified inside. We freeze, feel ice-cold, frozen, and prefer to look away, not wanting or being able to meet the situation head on. With respect to Medusa, such inner sensations are "consistent" and authentic, as this goddess is a monster who renders us lifeless. The myth tells us how humans can deal with this petrifying danger, namely like the Greek hero Perseus, who defeated Medusa by not looking at her directly, but at her reflection in a mirror. In analogy to this strategy, not becoming too preoccupied with the "shock" of the disease or not diving into online research to obtain in-depth information can sometimes be the right approach. This could also illustrate why some cancer patients prefer to schedule psychotherapy appointments every two to four weeks rather than on a weekly basis. They need to distance themselves from their illness, as looking too closely would make them feel uncomfortable. On a psychological level, dealing with dreams or inner images can also be understood as not looking directly, as the unconscious comments on the illness, so to speak, and this would seem an appropriate attitude to observe. If Medusa is seen as an archetypal image still valid and relevant to cancer today, which discloses something about the typical human mental experience of this disease, then the instinctive way in which patients and healthy persons keep their distance from each other would not be primarily inhuman or reprehensible, but based on a deeply rooted intuitive shyness. The myth even tells us that we must avert our gaze when faced with the danger of petrification.

Cancer patients who experience social distancing at first hand tragically misunderstand the behavior of healthy people towards them, concluding that there is something wrong with themselves, and that they might even come across as a monster – as described by 10-year-old leukemia sufferer Oscar in the novel "Oscar and the Lady in Pink". Upon learning that their son's bone marrow transplant has failed and that he will die soon, his parents are completely overwhelmed. They feel unable to face the brutal truth, do not want Oscar to know about it and lack the courage to let him see their pain and fear. Oscar overhears their conversation with the doctor and begins to hate his parents because they are afraid of behaving freely in his company. A grandmother called Rosa is the first to make him realize what is really going on, explaining that his parents are not afraid of him, but of the disease. He is not the monster, cancer is (Schmitt 2007, 85). This fictional narrative gets to the heart of the difficulties and misunderstandings that may arise in relationships between cancer patients and others. Some healthy people seek to hide their discomfort to avoid being petrified when confronted with another person's cancer diagnosis, which in turn results in awkwardness during meetings and complicated avoidance strategies.

Averting one's gaze from the petrifying Medusa could also be seen as a mythical representation of some cancer patients' tendency to deny the truth, downplay their illness, even steadfastly declare that their diagnosis is false, thus once again confirming this image. Fritz Meerwein, who compiled a wealth of psychosomatic studies on cancer in the 1970s, was able to demonstrate that an attitude of active denial can sometimes be associated with a good prognosis (Meerwein 1981, 120). His findings were backed up by a meta-analysis of 70 prospective psychoneuroimmunological studies carried out in 2004 (Schubert 2015c, 90). Hence, looking away can be beneficial – in line with the myth of Medusa. Such a defensive attitude is certainly not to be recommended, but hints at the fact that these strange-seeming study results have a counterpart in ancient imagery. I have on several occasions met people who have refused to acknowledge their clinically diagnosed cancer and have then gone on to live a better and significantly longer life than the medical statistics would indicate. In all these cases, the patients' denial was based on a rock-solid conviction that they did not have cancer and this deep belief rendered them free from fear. As repeatedly mentioned, this belief and freedom from fear have a positive physical influence and are eminently important for a healthy, balanced immune system, which could at least partially explain how this phenomenon occurs. A "superficial" or half-hearted denial of one's illness will therefore not bring about the desired positive effect. If we consider the image of Medusa when dealing with cancer, then it remains a matter of "when" and "how" we look at or confront this disease.

The hard shell of the hermit crab also had a symbolic significance for alchemists. Oncologists engage in intensive efforts to prolong the lives of their patients, and fight to cure and defeat cancer. However, despite the effective treatments available, such as surgery, chemotherapy and radiation, the disease still remains fatal for 50% of those affected. Could the shell of the crab be seen as a symbol for the resistance and tenacity which the disease shows in withstanding today's radical medical efforts? A historical note on this relates to Galen, who distinguished between benign and malignant tumors in the second century AD. In concordance with Hippocrates, he determined that one should generally not intervene in cancer with a scalpel, a recommendation that is no longer applicable today. However, a worsening of the disease or forming of metastases are occasionally described as being surgery-related. Psychoneuroimmunological studies have shown that damage to the vagus nerve plays a central role here (Schubert, 2015c, 106) and that stress-induced elevated catecholamines have an impact on the development of surgery-related metastases in lung tumors (Malarkey et. al. 2015, 44). Again, the effect of a person's emotional state on the physical healing process becomes evident here.

So far, I have presented only the somber aspects of cancer in the context of animal symbolism. If cancer is indeed an archetypal phenomenon, there would also have to be a brighter side, because an archetype is fundamentally paradoxical. The ability of hermit crabs to change their shells and their associated resurrection is one such positive image from the point of view of ancient scholars. The animal discards its shell whenever it starts to constrict and limit its growth, and the change in shell serves its development and coming to maturity. However, the old shell must first be broken for the "old" life to be finished before it can be renewed, i.e., "resurrected". Becoming new thus requires a sacrifice, namely the old shell, which must be given up. During this process, there is a dangerous transition period during which the new shell has not yet been formed, leaving the animal unprotected. If we were to translate this imagery, it could signify the existential threat of the disease, which can force or encourage affected persons to radically give up their previous habits and patterns of life, that is, to discard their "old shell". In this context, a "sacrifice" would mean rejecting an overly heroic attitude or an inappropriate adjustment, but could also refer to people who are overly courageous or carry too great a burden. They are used to persevering no matter what the cost, and such heroism must sometimes be sacrificed. It might also be a matter of no longer doing just what others expect of you, and what ultimately must be sacrificed is quite individual and varies considerably. It has to be worked out by instinct and put into practice with courage by those concerned without any guarantee of success. Whosoever sacrifices something and then manages to reorient themselves can, in the best case, find a new shell, a different kind of security, figuratively speaking. A difficult, sometimes even chaotic and dangerous period of reorientation may lie between the old and the new shell. If patients subsequently say that they needed their illness to save them, then the reorientation process triggered by their cancer has been a success.

5.5 The Cancer Evil: The Archetypal and the Personal Shadow

Buddha did not fight evil directly. When 20,000 demons set out rattling their sabers to kill him, they found only his empty lotus seat and were disappointed to discover that Buddha had simply retreated – without a fight. "The King's Son and the Devil's Daughter" (Zaunert 1976, 83) is a fairy tale about a likewise successful escape, and describes the circumstances under which people can flee from the devil, who over the epochs has represented the respective collective evil. Playing a symbolic role in cancer, the devil is occasionally visible in attributions on an unconscious level. Those who experience oncology departments as "total hell," for example, will hardly deny the symbolic proximity of cancer, cancer treatment, and the devil.

The aforementioned fairy tale begins with a life-weary king, who has lost a war and receives unexpected help from a stranger. As in similar stories, the king promises the stranger the reward asked for, *en noa Sil* (a new soul), unaware that this means his newborn son. After twenty-one years, the man, who is none other than the devil, comes to collect his reward. The devil commands the king's son to drain a pond during the night and to bring in a huge crop of hay, otherwise he will be thrown into hellfire. The king's son cries because he knows that he is not up to the task and thus, must die. When the devil's daughter spies the sad youth, her heart is stirred, and she promises to help him. She secretly summons the spirits of hell during the night to do all the work. The devil is astonished and grim-faced in the morning when he sees the work has been done. The king's son is now given a far more difficult job, which the infernal spirits also take on. At this point, the devil becomes suspicious and offers the king's son his freedom should he succeed in building a church of pure sand during the coming night. However, despite all their efforts, the infernal spirits do not succeed, whereupon the devil's daughter transforms herself into a white horse so that the king's son may flee. When the spirits of hell confess the next morning that they helped the young man at the daughter's behest, the enraged devil orders them to capture the two fugitives dead or alive. On the run, the daughter manages to outwit the infernal spirits three times by transforming herself and the king's son: firstly, into a church and a priest, then into an alder tree and a golden bird, and finally into a rice paddy and a quail. The infernal spirits having failed three times, the devil himself sets out in pursuit. When his daughter realizes this, she turns herself into a lake of milk and the prince into a duck, whom she orders to remain in the middle of the lake with his head dipped under. The devil now tries to lure the duck to the shore and after a while, the duck feels like looking over at him. It immediately goes blind and the milk becomes cloudy and begins to ferment. A voice cries out, "Woe, woe, what hast thou done?" At this, the devil dances for joy and shouts "I'll get you soon!". As the duck refuses to be lured to the shore, the angry devil turns himself into a goose and proceeds to drink the milk along with the duck. Now the milk starts to steam and curdle, the devil bursts and his daughter and the prince are left standing in the beauty of youth.

Within the context of cancer, the beginning and the end of the story are of primary interest. A fairy tale involving a king deals with a collectively relevant situation, because what affects the king, in turn affects his people. The problem thus concerns everyone. In the tale, the king did not initially suspect that the help offered to him to overcome his distress was not for free and that he would owe the devil by paying a price: initially fruitful and growth-promoting over a certain period of time (21 years), the devil's help now threatens to destroy the next generation when his son's life is put in danger. This image illustrates clearly that a destructive element, i.e., the collective shadow, may exist behind positive outcomes and progress, and although at first seemingly helpful, may exact its toll with the lapse of time. The synthetic form of estrogen known as DES (diethylstilbestrol) is a representative example of such a process. A popular drug in the 1950s, it was taken to prevent premature births and miscarriages. Around 1970, within the framework of a study, women with uterine cancer were asked whether they had ever taken estrogen. It was then revealed that it was not the cancer patients themselves, but their mothers who had taken the synthetic hormone DES and that the carcinoma had skipped a generation (Mukherjee 2010, 206).

If we revert to the fairytale, the danger posed by the devil manifests itself in the form of tasks that the prince cannot hope to solve by human strength alone. From a psychological perspective, the ego is not able to cope with the collective shadow all by itself. The situation becomes fatal when the prince is threatened with the loss of his life in hellfire if the impossible is not accomplished. Cancer patients experience something similar, namely the feeling that a malignant tumor is rampant and imperils their life. Personal will and human effort do not always suffice to overcome destructive forces. How can someone who feels threatened in this way seek help?

In the fairy tale, the prince is saved by the devil's daughter who displays human emotions. Touched by his tears and sorrow, and his powerlessness, she betrays her own father. In line with the fairy tale, feelings of grief, anger, or helplessness on the part of the cancer patient can mobilize super-personal psychic forces, as represented by the devil's daughter. It is imperative that the individual at risk trusts and obeys these forces, which guide the "Ego" towards contact with a feminine aspect of the dark self. Although this has a supporting and protective effect, helpful forces in the form of hell spirits and the devil's daughter are dark or shadow aspects. It is therefore probably true to conclude that the devil and evil can only be withstood if shadow forces are activated and acknowledged, and the individual does not insist on being "saintly". In reality, patients are then not quite as nice, amicable, or willing to compromise as they used to be. Spirits of hell can also be seen as an image symbolizing the sometimes brutal treatment methods, for example, the invasive medical procedures employed by the surgeon Halsted. He removed not only the breast, but the pectoral muscles, the thoracic wall, and occasionally the ribs, parts of the sternum or clavicle from women suffering from breast cancer. Revered as a "patron saint," few dared to criticize him for the endless suffering or "hell" which he put his cancer patients through. His procedures were mutilating and involved considerable physical impairment. In the aggressive fight against cancer, in the pursuit of victory over death, there lies the danger of becoming self-indulgent and overly brutal oneself – much like cancer itself. Not only the disease, but also the actual heroic fight against it are partly overshadowed by intemperance. And yet, cancer can rarely be defeated without a measure of brutality.

On the one hand, the fairy tale teaches us that in the face of the threat of evil, both escape and transformation are necessary, while on the other hand, it is important to distance oneself from collective evil. The various images of transformation provide clues as to which psychic forces resist the collective shadow, allowing time to be gained initially.

The images of the church and the priest remind us of the power of traditional prayer and faith, while the tree with a bird, the rice paddy and the quail are references to Great Mother Earth. Accordingly, prayers, rites of faith or a nature-based healthy lifestyle can help halt the destructive process, as confirmed in a well-known medical journal (*Deutsches Ärzteblatt*) more than 20 years ago: the results obtained from a study indicated the importance of spirituality and prayers in the healing process (Glomp 1997, 1368f). This is the reason why psychoanalyst Tilman Moser entreats us not to depreciate the religiosity of patients as a "dubious solution" from the outset. It is more a question of using therapy to open up a space within which to deal with all the feelings and thoughts related to God, including angry and reproachful ones (Moser 2017, 111).

The Byzantine Greek physician Paul of Aegina first described the effects of faith in the 7th century. He taught the art of cancer surgery, while pointing out that cancer patients must prepare themselves for the operation both mentally and by following an appropriate diet. Thus, a woman suffering from breast cancer should pray to St. Agatha, a Christian who was tortured around 250 AD under Emperor Decius because of her faith. Her breasts were torn off with pliers, and she was thrown into a dungeon without receiving any treatment. St. Peter is said to have appeared to her during the night to heal her terrible wounds. When women suffering from breast cancer invoke this martyr before their own breast surgery, converse with her, perhaps even identify with her, they are seeking help from divine healing powers, opening up to spiritual forces. To this day, people seek the proximity of individuals who have been healed: when the American Lance Armstrong once again set off in 2000 after his recovery from cancer to win the Tour de France, the most difficult cycling race in the world, numerous people with cancer lined his path, cheering on their idol. Both St. Agatha and Lance Armstrong inspired confidence in the face of the terrible, and these positive emotions are powerful, especially when surgery is imminent. The importance of such preoperative emotional factors has also been emphasized in recent psychoimmunological studies. It was demonstrated that experiencing preoperative emotional support and being able to rely on others has a positive effect on healing, whereas objective parameters, such as living together with a partner or children, do not (Schubert 2015c, 97).

In the fairy tale, the devil's destruction is initiated only after the prince, now transformed into a duck, disobeys the devil's daughter by looking at the devil rather than heeding her advice. As a result, the milk begins to ferment. Curiosity and "disobedience" seem to be the decisive factors here that lead to the furious devil finally being destroyed from within by the milk. For the cancer sufferer, this could signify that not listening to the advice of others might, under certain circumstances, destroy the cancer. At a decisive moment, an event breaks through the causal level – something surprising, incalculable, and unpredictable occurs at the very moment a decision is made. Spontaneous healings might be better understood in this way. A few years ago, an elderly man appeared on the television program "Miracles Happen" and spoke about the highly advanced state of his cancer: tumors had been found in his abdominal cavity, lungs, and liver. Doctors were no longer able to help him and sent him home to die. The man lost his appetite, he became steadily weaker and could no longer get dressed on his own. When he hit the lowest point in his life, he sat down and said to his wife that he thought it was high time to make a will. After this had been drawn up, he remarked that he had just felt something inside his body crack, as if something had broken. The patient felt relieved and from that day on, things started to look up and his malignant tumors regressed completely. Another young woman, commenting to a television crew on her illness, said that the doctors had given up treating her cancer. She had gone home and then said to herself, "You can't put your parents through this; it would not be okay to have them standing at your grave." This patient also experienced a spontaneous healing.

Whether any of the above behavior or attitudes were sufficient to bring about a spontaneous healing or be a deciding factor remains open. In my opinion, spontaneous healings are grace experienced, they happen unpredictably, come from the realm of the impossible and the unintended. From a psychological perspective, they are synchronistic events, making it impossible to give advice such as: "If you draw up your will, your cancer will be defeated." Spontaneous healing has nothing to do with knowing or doing something, it just happens in a mysterious way.

The German theologian Jakob Böhme said that life can only exist when good and evil stand side by side. Phrased in psychological terms, evil (even if manifested as cancer) can be seen as the starting point of the individuation process. Alchemists were the first to call the beginning of this process of self-discovery and self-awareness "nigredo", meaning darkness, which is accompanied by anxiety and depression. Many people going through depression have experienced external life as terribly troublesome, since nothing seems to go right and they lack the necessary energy. In a stricter sense, depression forces introspection, looking and listening to one's hidden inner world. We cannot anticipate what will ultimately emerge from nigredo, there is no guarantee or certainty, the nature of the soul and the collective unconscious are immeasurable.

Rapid advances in all walks of life and our ever-expanding knowledge often mean that we do not perceive and appreciate the miracle of life and divine creation in its numinous life-giving forms as much as we should. This is manifest by the way we handle both pregnancy and birth, for example. By increasingly placing new life into the care of doctors, birth has lost its mystery as an event, and our predetermined happiness is less noticeable and overwhelming. Perhaps that is why we encounter the numinous more frequently nowadays in the destructive elements which we are confronted with, and above all, trust and devotion are demanded of us in such situations.

Devotion and introversion are important, but given the right time and the right means, we must also dare to actively fight evil, as echoed by the Egyptian book of the underworld Amduat, written around 1500 BC and referred to as the "Text of the Hidden Chamber" (Schweizer 2010). Using the example of the journey of the sun god through the twelve hours of the night, it illustrates in symbolic images how everything that is old, worn, or weak must plunge into darkness in order to regenerate. The process always includes an encounter with evil, which may not be looked directly in the eye according to this myth, but must be fought with the sword at a very specific hour. The Amduat states that the fight with collective evil leads to the threshold of death, i.e., is life-threatening. In the case of cancer, we are aware of the risk of death that chemotherapy poses, as it can weaken the immune system in a critical way. This is quite drastic in patients suffering from leukemia, as their bone marrow becomes entirely destroyed by high-dose chemotherapy. They are brought to the very brink of death in a concrete and conscious manner, and without a successful bone marrow transplant from a donor, death is certain for patients treated in this way.

However, it is not only the sick, but also physicians who are confronted with their shadow when treating cancer. Faced with "incurable" cases, doctors and therapists may sometimes behave aggressively or even dismissively because they feel mortified by limitations which they find difficult to address on a conscious level. Physicians and their patients often become alienated from one other as a result of this process.

The following account illustrates how difficult it can be for doctors to deal in an appropriate manner with the despair and anger of a person suffering from cancer. A woman with breast cancer described the following: "After six cycles of chemotherapy, radiation therapy was due to continue without a break in between. The surgeon had on a previous occasion assured me that today's surgical methods would no longer cause lymphedema, as long as my armpit remained untreated. The radiation therapist, on the other hand, claimed that he could not make allowance for the surgeon's work and would have to irradiate my armpit, which might lead to lymphedema. Finding myself tossed about like a ping pong ball between the doctors and their opinions was unpleasant and demotivating as far as radiation was concerned. Something inside me rebelled. I was dead miserable and tired and just didn't want to go along with it anymore. I asked the doctor in charge of radiation therapy to prescribe some kind of vitamin or restorative, since I almost couldn't take it anymore. 'That won't be necessary,' decided the doctor. 'Make sure you get enough sleep and follow a healthy diet, that will be enough!' I had kept up my courage until then, but this proclamation caused me to waver. I burst into tears. Horrified at my weeping, the doctor became angry and said, 'I thought I was speaking with a grown-up woman, and here you are behaving like a child.

Don't be so stupid. You are doing well and coping fine with the chemo. Others have had to interrupt it.' I was trembling with rage inside. Three days before my radiation ended, a passing female doctor whom I did not know said, "I hear you are complaining again", even though she had no idea what the issue was about and didn't know me personally. I once more felt at the doctors' mercy and became very angry again. So I summoned up my strength and kicked the door through which the female doctor had disappeared with all my might. I hope she fell off her chair in fright! Unfortunately, I was unable to have an in-person conversation with the head physician, who merely ordered my treatment to be interrupted because of my troublemaking. My general practitioner intervened at that point, and I was able to have the final lot of radiation treatment."

Another tale is told about Thomas Lynch, a lung cancer specialist, who had the ability to sense anxiety in his cancer patients and take the time to inquire about their personal circumstances, future aspirations, and fears. He never glossed over the statistics and spoke openly to patients about the risks. He promised that should any complications arise, he would take care of them and explained how, whilst remaining realistic and refraining from the use of aggressive language (Mukherjee, 2010, 307f). According to all reports, he was an expert at dispelling his patients' fears.

Afterword

A short story to finish with: in 1995, twin sisters Kyrie and Brielle were born twelve weeks prematurely and placed in separate incubators in a critical condition. Kyrie's condition stabilized quickly, and she gained weight. Brielle fared much worse; she could barely breathe, had a pulse rate that was too high and blue-greyish skin. She also screamed a lot. When her condition deteriorated even further and Brielle was on the point of death, the attending nurse broke the clinical protocol and put the newborns together in one incubator. And something that no one could have foreseen happened: as soon as they were lying together, Kyrie immediately hugged her younger sister. As a result, Brielle gradually calmed down, her situation became stable – and she survived. The significance of bodily contact in the physical and emotional development of this prematurely born girl had become obvious. Today, the two sisters are healthy women (RTL.de, 2018).

Experiences such as these show how closely the body and psyche are interwoven. Much still remains a mystery in this regard, but we have already learnt a lot and there are other things which we have an inkling of. Some of the aspects of the relationship between the physical body and the psyche, the lived body and the soul, have been taken up and discussed in this book. The selection was subjective.

I would be pleased if this book aroused curiosity about the subject of psyche and soma, which affects all of us on a very personal level. Present on a daily basis, albeit mostly on an unconscious level, the topic has far-reaching consequences for our lifestyle, our relationships and our spirituality – which is why it is worth paying attention to.

Let me take this opportunity to thank everyone who has supported me directly and indirectly in my writing. A very special thanks goes to those who have allowed me to tell their story.

Literature

Abramovic, Marina. *Rhythm 0, 1974.* www.youtube.com/watch?v=eStK-DxzffZs. Last accessed on 30 May 2021.

Adler, Gerhard and Jaffé, Aniela, eds., *C.G. Jung Letters*, Volume 1, Bollingen Series, XCV: 1, Princeton: Princeton University Press, 1973.

Ammann, Ruth. *Die Sandspieltherapie. Resonanz zwischen Körper und Seele.* Gießen: Psychosozial, 2019.

Austin, Sue. *Working with Chronic and Relentless Self-Hatred, Self-Harm and Existential Shame: A Clinical Study and Reflections.* London: Journal of Analytical Psychology 61, 2016a.

Austin, Sue. *Working with Chronic and Relentless Self-Hatred, Self-Harm and Existential Shame: A Clinical Study and Reflections* (Paper 2 of 2). London: Journal of Analytical Psychology 61, 2016b.

Bach, Susan. *Life Paints its Own Span.* Einsiedeln: Daimon, 1990.

Benecke, Cord. *Negative Affekte in der Psychotherapie.* Stuttgart: Kohlhammer, 2018.

Benedetti, Fabrizio. *Placebo Effects.* Oxford: Oxford University Press, 2014.

Böhme, Gernot. *Leibsein als Aufgabe, Leibphilosophie in pragmatischer Sicht.* Zug: Prof. Dr. Alfred Schmid-Stiftung, 2003.

Broom, Brian C. Bedeutungs-*volle* Krankheit, Psychoneuroimmunologie und der *Mind-Body*-Arzt. In: Schubert, Christian (ed.), *Psychoneuroimmunologie und Psychotherapie.* Stuttgart: Schattauer, 2015.

Brothers Grimm. *Grimm's Complete Fairytales.* San Diego: Canterbury Classics/Baker & Taylor Publishing, 2011.

Bruch, Hilde. *The Golden Cage – The Enigma of Anorexia Nervosa.* Cambridge: Harvard University Press, 1978.

Canetti, Elias. *Crowds and Power.* New York: Farrar, Straus and Giroux, 1984.

Cousins, Norman. *Anatomy of an Illness: As Perceived by the Patient.* New York: W. W. Norton & Company, 2005.

Daniel, Renate. *Leib, Symbol, Archetyp.* In: Frick, Eckhard & Vogel, Ralf T. (eds.). Den Abschied vom Leben verstehen. Psychoanalyse und Palliative Care, 2017.

Daniel, Renate. *The Self. Quest for Meaning in a Changing World.* Einsiedeln: Daimon, 2020.

Damasio, Antonio. *The Feeling of what Happens. Body, Emotion and the Making of Consciousness.* London: Vintage Books, 2000.

Dethlefsen, Thorwald & Dahlke, Rüdiger. *The Healing Power of Illness: Understanding what your Symptoms are Telling You.* Boulder: Sentient Publications, 2016.

Dörner, Dietrich. *Bauplan für eine Seele.* Reinbek: Rowohlt, 2001.

Dorst, Brigitte, Vogel, Ralf (ed.). *Aktive Imagination. Schöpferisch leben aus inneren Bildern.* Stuttgart: Kohlhammer, 2014.

Ermann, Michael. *Psychotherapie und Psychosomatik. Ein Lehrbuch auf psychoanalytischer Grundlage.* Stuttgart: Kohlhammer, 2016.

Fuchs, Thomas. *Leib und Lebenswelt. Neue philosophisch-psychiatrische Essays.* Zug: Prof. Dr. Alfred Schmid-Stiftung, 2008.

Floridi, Luciano. *The 4th Revolution. How the Infosphere is Reshaping Human Reality.* Oxford: Oxford University Press, 2014.

Fonagy, Peter, Gergely, György, Jurist, Elliot L. & Target, Mary. *Affect Regulation, Mentalization, and the Development of the Self.* New York: Other Press, 2002.

Geisenhanslüke, Ralph. *Kein Organ wie jedes andere.* Geo Wissen Gesundheit 11. Hamburg: G+J Medien GmbH, 2019.

Glomp, Ingrid. *Das Phänomen der unerwarteten Genesung.* Deutsches Ärzteblatt (25), 20 June 1997.

Gramich, Bernd. *Psychosomatische Krankheit als Entwicklungshemmung: Überwindung – Chronifizierung – Tod. Betrachtungen am Beispiel der Essstörungen.* Analytische Psychologie. Zeitschrift für Psychotherapie und Psychoanalyse. Frankfurt: Brandes & Apsel, 2019.

Horn, Andrea B., Mehl, Matthias R., & große Deters, Fenne. Expressives Schreiben und Immunaktivität – gesundheitsfördernde Aspekte der Selbstöffnung. In: Schubert, Christian (ed.), *Psychoneuroimmunologie und Psychotherapie.* Stuttgart: Schattauer, 2015.

Jaffé, Aniela (ed.). *Memories, Dreams, Reflections by C.G. Jung.* New York: Pantheon Books, 1973.

Jaffé, Aniela. *The Myth of Meaning in the Work of C.G. Jung.* Einsiedeln: Daimon, 1984.

Jung, C.G. *Ein Brief zur Frage der Synchronizität.* Zeitschrift für Parapsychologie und Grenzgebiete der Psychologie 5, 1961.

Jung, Carl Gustav. *Collected Works. Volume 18/1.* Princeton: Princeton University Press, 1976.

Jung, Carl Gustav. *Collected Works. Volume 11.* Princeton: Princeton University Press, 1958.

Jung, Carl Gustav. *Collected Works. Volume 13.* Princeton: Princeton University Press, 1967.

Jung, Carl Gustav. *Collected Works. Volume 7.* Princeton: Princeton University Press, 1966.

Jung, Carl Gustav. *Collected Works. Volume 12.* Princeton: Princeton University Press, 1968.

Jung, Carl Gustav. *Collected Works. Volume 14/2.* Princeton: Princeton University Press, 1963.

Jung, Carl Gustav. *Letters, Volume I, 1906-1950.* Selected and edited by Gerhard Adler in collaboration with Aniela Jaffé. Princeton: Princeton University Press, 1973.

Jung, Carl Gustav. *Collected Works. Volume 2.* Princeton: Princeton University Press, 1972.

Jung, Carl Gustav. *Collected Works. Volume 8.* Princeton: Princeton University Press, 1969.

Jung, Carl Gustav. *Collected Works. Volume 9/1.* Princeton: Princeton University Press, 1959.

Jung, Carl Gustav. *Collected Works. Volume 9/2.* Princeton: Princeton University Press, 1959.

Jung, Carl Gustav. *Collected Works. Volume 6.* Princeton: Princeton University Press, 1971.

Jung, Carl Gustav. *Collected Works. Volume 16.* Princeton: Princeton University Press, 1985.

C.G. Jung beantwortet Fragen 4/6, 1958. https://youtu.be/UoSo0gPWHQ8. Last accessed on 4 November 2021.

Kafka, Franz. *A Hunger Artist.* Rockville: Wildside Press, 2016.

Kalbitzer, Jan. *Das Geschenk der Sterblichkeit. Wie die Angst vor dem Tod zum Sinn des Lebens führen kann.* München: Blessing, 2018.

Kalsched, Don. *Trauma and the Soul A psycho-spiritual approach to human development and its interruption.* London: Routledge, 2013.

Kast, Verena. *The Dynamics of Symbols. Fundamentals of Jungian Psychotherapy.* New York: Fromm International, 1992.

Kast, Verena. *Abschied von der Opferrolle. Das eigene Leben leben.* Freiburg: Herder, 1998.

Kast, Verena. *Imagination. Zugänge zu inneren Ressourcen finden.* Ostfildern: Patmos, 2016.

Kast, Verena. Komplexe und ihre Kompensation. Anregungen aus der affektiven Neurowissenschaft. In: *Analytische Psychologie. Zeitschrift für Psychotherapie und Psychoanalyse, 191.* Frankfurt: Brandes & Apsel, *2019.*

Kerényi, Karl. *Urbilder der griechischen Religion.* Stuttgart Klett-Cotta, 1998.

Kirschner, Monika. *Wunder sind möglich. Heilungschancen bei Krebspatienten.* WDR, 22 September 1997.

Kucklick, Christoph. *Die granulare Gesellschaft. Wie das Digitale unsere Wirklichkeit auflöst.* Berlin: Ullstein, 2014.

Küchenhoff, Joachim & Wiegerling, Klaus. *Leib und Körper.* Göttingen: Vandenhoeck & Ruprecht, 2008.

Kraft, Hartmut. *Grenzgänger zwischen Kunst und Psychiatrie.* Köln: DuMont, 1986.

Kremer, Dennis. Es geht auch ohne Kreditkarte. *Frankfurter Allgemeine Sonntagzeitung, 2013.*

Lier, Doris. *Totentanz. Bilder einer magersüchtigen Zeit.* Zürich: IKM Guggenbühl AG, 2001.

Maio, Giovanni. *Mittelpunkt Mensch: Ethik in der Medizin.* Stuttgart: Schattauer, 2012.

Malarkey, William B., Tafur, Joseph R., Rutledge, Thomas & Mills, Paul J. Neuroendokrinologie und Psychoneuroimmunologie. In: Christian Schubert (ed.), *Psychoneuroimmunologie und Psychotherapie.* Stuttgart: Schattauer, 2015.

Meerwein, Fritz (ed.). *Einführung in die Psycho-Onkologie.* Bern: Hans Huber, 1981.

Meier, Carl A. *Experiment und Symbol.* Olten: Walter, 1975.

Meier, Carl A. *Die Bedeutung des Traumes.* Olten: Walter, 1979.

Meier, Carl A. *Die Empirie des Unbewussten. Mit besonderer Berücksichtigung des Assoziationsexperimentes von C.G. Jung.* Zürich: Daimon, 1994.

Morris, David B. *The Culture of Pain.* Berkeley/Los Angeles: University of California Press, 1991.

Moser, Tilmann. *Raum für die Neuerfahrung Gottes. Aus der Arbeit eines Psychoanalytikers.* Spiritual Care, 6(1), 2017.

Mukherjee, Siddhartha. *The Emperor of All Maladies: A Biography of Cancer.* New York: Simon & Schuster, 2010.

Niggermann, Bernd & Zänker, Kurt S. Immunologische Grundlagen der Psychoneuroimmunologie. In: Schubert, Christian (ed.), *Psychoneuroimmunologie und Psychotherapie.* Stuttgart: Schattauer, 2015.

Panksepp, Jaak & Biven, Lucy. *The Archaeology of Mind. Neuroevolutionary Origins of Human Emotions.* New York: W. Norton & Company, 2012.

Picardi, Angelo, Tarsitani, Lorenzo, Tarolla, Emanuele & Biondi, Massimo. Negativfaktoren, Immunaktivität und Psychotherapie. In: Schubert, Christian (ed.), *Psychoneuroimmunologie und Psychotherapie.* Stuttgart: Schattauer, 2015.

RTL.de. *Frühchen rettete Schwester*: www.rtl.de/cms/fruehchen-rettete-schwester-durch-eine-umarmung-so-geht-es-den-zwillingen-heute-2597113.html, 17 January 2018. Last accessed on 29 August 2021

Roth, Gerhard & Strüber, Nicole. *Wie das Gehirn die Seele macht.* Stuttgart: Klett-Cotta, 2014.

Schipperges, Heinrich. *Krankheit und Kranksein im Spiegel der Geschichte.* Berlin: Springer, 1999.

Schmitt, Eric-Emmanuel. *Oskar und die Dame in Rosa.* Frankfurt: Fischer, 2007.

Schubert, Christian (ed.). *Psychoneuroimmunologie und Psychotherapie.* Stuttgart: Schattauer, 2015.

Schubert, Christian. *Vorwort zur zweiten Auflage.* Schubert, Christian (ed.). Psychoneuroimmunologie und Psychotherapie. Stuttgart: Schattauer, 2015a.

Schubert, Christian. *Einführung.* In: Christian Schubert (ed.). Psychoneuroimmunologie und Psychotherapie. Stuttgart: Schattauer, 2015b.

Schubert, Christian. *Psychoeuroimmunologie körperlicher Erkrankungen.* In: Schubert, Christian (ed). Psychoneuroimmunologie und Psychotherapie. Stuttgart: Schattauer, 2015c.

Schubert, Christian, Exenberger, Silvia. *Einfluss von frühen psychischen Belastungen auf die Entwicklung von Entzündungserkrankungen im Erwachsenenalter.* In: Schubert, Christian (ed.). Psychoneuroimmunologie und Psychotherapie. Stuttgart: Schattauer, 2015.

Schubert, Christian, Amberger, Madeleine. *Was uns krank macht, was uns heilt. Aufbruch in eine neue Medizin. Das Zusammenspiel von Körper, Geist und Seele besser verstehen.* Munderfing: Fischer & Gann, 2019.

Schweizer, Andreas. *The Sungod's Journey through the Netherworld: Reading the Ancient Egyptian Amduat.* Cornell: Cornell University Press, 2010.

Skloot, Rebecca. *The Immortal Life of Henrietta Lacks.* New York: Crown Publishing Group, 2011.

Solms, Marc, and Oliver Turnbull. *The Brain and the Inner World: An Introduction to the Neuroscience of the Subjective Experience.* New York: Other Press, 2003.

Sontag, Susan. *Illness as a Metaphor.* New York: Farrar, Straus & Giroux, 1978.

Spektrum der Wissenschaft. Spezial 5: *Krebsmedizin, 1996.*

Strobel, Hermann. *Das Zahnweh subjektiv genommen: Über Zähne, Zahnschmerzen, Zahnärzte, und ihre Bedeutung für den Seelenfrieden.* Olten: Walter, 1990.

Stockrahm, Sven. *Angelina Jolies zweiter Versuch, dem Krebs zu entkommen.* www.zeit.de/wissen/gesundheit/2015-03/angelina-jolie-krebs-eierstoecke-entfernung, 2015. Last accessed on 27 August 2021.

The Holy Bible. *Old and New Testament. King James Version.* New York: Harper Collins, 2011.

Toellner, Richard. *Illustrierte Geschichte der Medizin.* Erlangen: Karl Müller, 1992.

van Heyst, Ilse. *Das Schlimmste war die Angst.* Frankfurt/Main: Fischer, 1982.

van Lommel, Pim. *Endloses Bewusstsein. Neue medizinische Fakten zur Nahtoderfahrung.* Ostfildern: Patmos, 2014.

van Lommel, Pim. *Consciousness Beyond Life: The Science of the Near-Death Experience.* New York: Harper One, 2011.

von Franz, Marie-Louise. *On Dreams and Death. A Jungian Interpretation.* Boston/London: Shambhala Publications, 1986.

von Franz, Marie-Louise. *Shadow and Evil in Fairy Tales.* Boulder: Shambhala Publications, 1995.

von Franz, Marie-Louise. *Psyche and Matter.* Boston/London: Shambhala Publications, 1992.

von Franz, Marie-Louise. *Archetypal Dimensions of the Psyche.* Boston/London: Shambhala Publications, 1999.

von Franz, Marie-Louise. *The Cat. A Tale of Feminine Redemption.* Toronto: Inner City Books, 2000.

von Glasenapp, Helmuth. *Die fünf Weltreligionen.* München: Diederichs, 1995.

Weinreb, Friedrich. *Der siebenarmige Leuchter.* Weiler im Allgäu: Thauros, 1985.

Weinreb, Friedrich. *Leiblichkeit. Unser Körper und seine Organe als Ausdruck des ewigen Menschen.* Weiler im Allgäu: Thauros, 1987.

Weinreb Friedrich. *Vom Sinn des Erkrankens. Gesundsein und Krankwerden.* Bern: Origo, 1999.

Whitmont, Edward. *The Alchemy of Healing.* Berkeley: North Atlantic Books, 1993.

Whitmont, Edward C. & Perera, Sylvia Brinton. *Dreams, A Portal to the Source.* London/New York: Routledge, 1989.

Winnicott, Donald W. *Playing and Reality.* New York: Routledge, 1997.

Zaunert, Paul (ed.). *Die verwunschene Prinzessin.* In: Deutsche Märchen seit Grimm. Jena: Eugen Diederichs, 1919.

Zaunert, Paul (ed.). *Der Königssohn und die Teufelstochter* In: Deutsche Märchen seit Grimm. Jena: Eugen Diederichs, 1919.

Zellermayer, Ofer. *The Pain of Paying.* ResearchGate, 1996. Last accessed on 4 November 2021. www.researchgate.net/publication/280711796_The_Pain_of_Paying.

Zimmer, Heinrich. *Der Weg zum Selbst. Lehre und Leben des indischen Heiligen Shri Ramana Maharshi aus Tiruvannamalei.* Zürich: Rascher, 1954.

Ziegler Alfred. *Archetypal Medicine.* Washington: Spring Publications, 2000.

By the same Author

Renate Daniel

The Self: Quest for Meaning in a Changing World

Whoever engages in C.G. Jung's concept of the self will be confronted with questions relating to humanity, and concepts of God, the divine and faith. Jung deems it necessary to treat these topics on a psychological level because of the far-reaching implications they have on the way we live and relate to each other. But they also impact on ethical attitudes, ideologies, social processes and therapeutic models. Scientific evidence usually proves difficult. A certain open-mindedness towards this topic is expected on the part of the reader, and it would be helpful to embrace the ideas put forward 'without prejudice' for the moment. This book aims to help readers become more aware of their own ideas and convictions and how these may influence one's self-image and worldview.

164 pages, ISBN 978-3-85630-781-3

Taking the Fear Out of the Night - Coping with Nightmares

Anyone who is plagued by nightmares night after night knows what a heavy burden these nocturnal apparitions represent: one is unable to resume sleep, often lies awake for a long time, and feels fearful, irritable or depressed the next day.

What can help to take the fear out of the night?

Understanding the message of nightmares is a first step toward relief. These energy-laden images can represent urgent questions stemming from the depth of the psyche. In this book, experienced Jungian analyst Renate Daniel demonstrates how one can succeed in finding appropriate answers to help understand and cope with nightmares.

174 pages, ISBN 978-3-85630-760-8

English Titles from Daimon

Ruth Ammann - *The Enchantment of Gardens*
Susan R. Bach - *Life Paints its Own Span*
Diana Baynes Jansen - *Jung's Apprentice: A Biography of Helton Godwin Baynes*
John Beebe (Ed.) - *Terror, Violence and the Impulse to Destroy*
E.A. Bennet - *Meetings with Jung*
W.H. Bleek / L.C. Lloyd (Ed.) - *Specimens of Bushman Folklore*
Tess Castleman - *Threads, Knots, Tapestries*
- *Sacred Dream Circles*
Renate Daniel - *Taking the Fear out of the Night*
- *The Self: Quest for Meaning in a Changing World*
- *Psyche and Soma*
Eranos Yearbook 69 - *Eranos Reborn*
Eranos Yearbook 70 - *Love on a Fragile Thread*
Eranos Yearbook 71 - *Beyond Masters*
Eranos Yearbook 72 - *Soul between Enchantment and Disenchantment*
Eranos Yearbook 73 - *The World and its Shadow*
Eranos Yearbook 74 - *The Age of Immediacy at the Test of Meaning*
Michael Escamilla - *Bleuler, Jung, and the Schizophrenias*
Heinrich Karl Fierz - *Jungian Psychiatry*
John Fraim - *Battle of Symbols*
Liliane Frey-Rohn - *Friedrich Nietzsche, A Psychological Approach*
Marion Gallbach - *Learning from Dreams*
Ralph Goldstein (Ed.) - *Images, Meanings & Connections: Essays in Memory of Susan Bach*
Yael Haft - *Hands: Archetypal Chirology*
Irene & Andreas Gerber - *Encounters with C.G. Jung. The Journal of Sabi Tauber*
Fred Gustafson - *The Black Madonna of Einsiedeln*
Daniel Hell - *Soul-Hunger: The Feeling Human Being and the Life-Sciences*
Siegmund Hurwitz - *Lilith, the first Eve*
Aniela Jaffé - *The Myth of Meaning*
- *Was C.G. Jung a Mystic?*
- *From the Life and Work of C.G. Jung*
- *Death Dreams and Ghosts*
C.G. Jung - *The Solar Myths and Opicinus de Canistris*
Verena Kast - *A Time to Mourn*
- *Sisyphus*
Hayao Kawai - *Dreams, Myths and Fairy Tales in Japan*
James Kirsch - *The Reluctant Prophet*
Eva Langley-Dános - *Prison on Wheels: Ravensbrück to Burgau*
Rivkah Schärf Kluger - *The Gilgamesh Epic*
Yehezkel Kluger & *Nomi Kluger-Nash* - *RUTH in the Light of Mythology, Legend and Kabbalah*
Paul Kugler (Ed.) - *Jungian Perspectives on Clinical Supervision*
Paul Kugler - *The Alchemy of Discourse*
Rafael López-Pedraza - *Cultural Anxiety*
- *Hermes and his Children*
Alan McGlashan - *The Savage and Beautiful Country*
- *Gravity & Levity*
Gregory McNamee (Ed.) - *The Girl Who Made Stars: Bushman Folklore*
- *The North Wind and the Sun & Other Fables of Aesop*
Gitta Mallasz / Hanna Dallos - *Talking with Angels*
C.A. Meier - *Healing Dream and Ritual*
- *A Testament to the Wilderness*
- *Personality: The Individuation Process*
Haruki Murakami - *Haruki Murakami Goes to Meet Hayao Kawai*

English Titles from Daimon

Eva Pattis Zoja (Ed.) - *Sandplay Therapy*
Laurens van der Post - *The Rock Rabbit and the Rainbow*
Jane Reid - *Jung, My Mother and I: The Analytic Diaries of Catharine Rush Cabot*
R.M. Rilke - *Duino Elegies*
A. Schweizer / R. Schweizer-Vüllers - *Stone by Stone: Reflections on Jung*
- *Wisdom has Built her House*
Miguel Serrano - *C.G. Jung and Hermann Hesse*
Helene Shulman - *Living at the Edge of Chaos*
D. Slattery / G. Slater (Eds.) - *Varieties of Mythic Experience*
David Tacey - *Edge of the Sacred: Jung, Psyche, Earth*
Susan Tiberghien - *Looking for Gold*
Ann Ulanov - *Spiritual Aspects of Clinical Work*
- *The Female Ancestors of Christ*
- *Healing Imagination*
- *Picturing God*
- *Receiving Woman*
- *Spirit in Jung*
- *The Wisdom of the Psyche*
- *The Wizards' Gate, Picturing Consciousness*
- *The Psychoid, Soul and Psyche*
- *Knots and their Untying*
Ann & Barry Ulanov - *Cinderella and her Sisters*
Eva Wertenschlag-Birkhäuser - *Windows on Eternity: The Paintings of Peter Birkhäuser*
Harry Wilmer - *How Dreams Help*
- *Quest for Silence*
Luigi Zoja - *Drugs, Addiction and Initiation*
Luigi Zoja & Donald Williams - *Jungian Reflections on September 11*
Jungian Congress Papers - *Jerusalem 1983: Symbolic & Clinical Approaches*
- *Berlin 1986: Archetype of Shadow in a Split World*
- *Paris 1989: Dynamics in Relationship*
- *Chicago 1992: The Transcendent Function*
- *Zürich 1995: Open Questions*
- *Florence 1998: Destruction and Creation*
- *Cambridge 2001*
- *Barcelona 2004: Edges of Experience*
- *Cape Town 2007: Journeys, Encounters*
- *Montreal 2010: Facing Multiplicity*
- *Copenhagen 2013: 100 Years on*
- *Kyoto 2016: Anima Mundi in Transition*
- *Vienna 2019: Encountering the Other*

Our books are available from your bookstore or from our distributors:

Baker & Taylor
30 Amberwood Parkway
Ashland OH 44805, USA
Phone: 419-281-5100
Fax: 419-281-0200
www.btpubservices.com

Gazelle Book Services Ltd.
White Cross Mills, High Town
Lancaster LA1 4XS, UK
Tel: +44 1524 528500
Email: sales@gazellebookservices.co.uk
www.gazellebookservices.co.uk

Daimon Verlag - Hauptstrasse 85 - CH-8840 Einsiedeln - Switzerland
Phone: (41)(55) 412 2266
Email: info@daimon.ch
Visit our website: **www.daimon.ch** or write for our complete catalog

www.ingramcontent.com/pod-product-compliance
Lightning Source LLC
LaVergne TN
LVHW091419190726
843491LV00006B/1500
* 9 7 8 3 8 5 6 3 0 7 8 7 5 *